AGING AS
COUNTERCULTURE

Earlier Books by David J. Maitland

Against the Grain: Coming Through Mid-Life Crisis, 1981

Looking Both Ways: A Theology for Mid-Life, 1985

Aging: A Time for New Learning, 1987

Aging As Counterculture

A Vocation for the Later Years

David J. Maitland

The Pilgrim Press

New York

Unless otherwise noted, scripture quotations are from the New Revised Standard Version Bible, copyright 1989, Division of Christian Education of the National Council of the Churches of Christ in the United States of America, and are used by permission. Brief quotations from the following versions are also used as indicated: Jerusalem Bible (JB), New English Bible (NEB), and The New Testament in Modern English, translated by J. B. Phillips (Phillips).

Permission is also gratefully acknowledged to the Association for Creative Change for the use of the material in chapter 1, "Spirituality in Aging: Regaining One's Balance," which first appeared in *Creative Change: Journal of Religion and Applied Behavioral Sciences*.

Library of Congress Cataloging-in-Publication Data

Maitland, David Johnston, 1922–
    Aging as counterculture : a vocation for the later years / J. Maitland.
       p. cm.
    Includes bibliographical references.
    ISBN 0-8298-0869-8 : $11.95
    1. Aged—Religious life. 2. Life style. I. Title.
BV4580.M284   1990
261.8'3426—dc20
                                   90-7837
                                    CIP

To the honor of
four distinguished
Presidents of Carleton College
1956–1986

Laurence M. Gould

John W. Nason

Howard R. Swearer

Robert E. Edwards

who, by varied encouragements,
enabled me to move toward understanding
ministry in the academy.

Contents

Preface

Apart from an idea attributed to Maggie Kuhn by an interviewer—that those who embrace the society most uncritically will have the most serious problems with aging—I must take full responsibility for what appears in this book. That interviewer's suggestion, however, opened me radically to an unfamiliar approach to familiar questions. For that, as for a vast variety of instructions by distinguished teachers and writers on subjects other than gerontology, I am grateful. I hope that I have not grossly or repeatedly misused biblical lessons learned long ago. What I have been doing for as long as two decades has been to pay ever-closer attention to my own experience as a possible source of spiritual understanding. More than I once could have imagined possible, I recognize today the wisdom in the adage "Necessity is the mother of invention."

These are among the chief obstacles, convictions, and hopes that run through the following chapters. After the opening discussion of my understanding of spirituality, I describe my beliefs about the inseparability of faith and experience. The penchant for order and the inescapable disorder of experience must both be embraced and taught to "dance" together to a variety of tunes and tempos. Though both seek preeminence and each has such power from time to time, in a healthy life neither may control permanently. From this somewhat unfamiliar clarification we move in the third chapter to an understanding of the forward impetus of what C. G. Jung refers to as "life's morning." During these decades both past and even present give way to the imperiousness of future preoccupations. It is here that the powers and limitations of adulthood's concentrations are to be seen.

Since such a narrowed understanding of human needs and experience is widespread, we turn in Chapter 4 to the work of those aging who, having long preferred activity over reflection, as society urges, find that they need to reclaim something of the life they have lived. Although they may not even be remembered, events unintegrated into the individual's self-understanding continue to act out their destructive and/or self-destructive consequences. Among aging's central tasks, which require one to make a place for recollection and reflection, is to recover and assume responsibility for one's life to date. Unclaimed lives will not be sources of blessing.

Chapter 5, "Aging as Counterculture," constitutes the heart of the book. There the case is made that, as their outlooks almost unavoidably change with the passage of time, older people find themselves increasingly uninterested in the exhortations and lures of their younger years. In tandem with this loss of interest in so-called popular things, older people often sense new interests attempting to surface. This tension is fraught with spiritual peril and promise. One either begins to pretend interest in what was earlier absorbing or, knowing pretense to be spiritually lethal, gradually takes an ever more adversarial stance against a society that affirms too little of the human potential.

In the last chapter, "Aging As God's Design," I attempt to give the most positive interpretation possible of growing older. I know that all eras and people in all traditions have acknowledged ambivalent feelings about aging. I have them myself. Although I may be criticized for a romantic one-sidedness, I reject the charge and defend the imbalance. In a society with such distorted views of aging as characterize our time, I concluded that only an extremely opposite stance had any chance of being heard. Since my desire is to effect needed change, I write about aging as counterculture. By assuming such a stance, older people have a chance of discovering a vocation worthy of life's later years.

In attempting throughout to understand human experience
sub specie aeternitatis I have intended to proceed as a person of
faith to whom some intelligence was given. More often than
not I have favored an indirect approach to matters of religious
belief. In the Epilogue, however, the reader is reminded that
the questions which surface in later life are usually inherently
religious. The emerging awareness of one's mortality is often
distinctly instructive.

If this quest for a vocation in later life turns out not to be
one of God's blessings, I have been looking in the wrong place
for evidences of that grace. That I have searched persistently
may be seen in two pieces written about a decade apart: "In
Praise of Aging," in my first book, *Against the Grain: Coming
Through Mid-Life Crisis* (New York: Pilgrim Press, 1981), and
the more recent book *Aging: A Time for New Learning*, (Louisville: The Westminster/John Knox Press, 1987). Especially
since the latter was published there have been stimulating
invitations to reflect publicly about matters related to aging,
and often about the relationship of faith and the experience of
growing older. While I am incapable of being specific about my
gains, I know that I learned much from these recent teaching
opportunities: during Lent of 1987, at the Westmoreland
United Church of Christ, Bethesda, Maryland; in late spring
of 1988, three lectures at the Westminster Presbyterian
Church, Minneapolis; at a stimulating day-long conference,
"Aging by God's Design," in October 1988, at the First Congre-
gational Church, UCC, Battle Creek, Michigan; and a lecture,
"Aging As a Spiritual Crisis," at the annual Minnesota Senior
Options '88 in St. Paul. Without holding any of these institutions responsible for my views, I recognize the opportunity for
personal maturation in their gracious invitations. Particular
thanks are due to Gordon Forbes, Elizabeth Heller, and David
Graham, ministers in their respective churches. I also want to
thank the Reverend James Slocum for his critical reading of an
earlier version of the Introduction to this book; and to Harold
L. Twiss for editing the entire manuscript.

It would be graceless to conclude these expressions of indebtedness without speaking about certain local encouragement.

Roy Elveton, academic dean of the college from which I received so much over three decades, granted a small amount of money which wound up in the pocket of a recent Carleton alumnus. It was a former student, Dean Nasby, '88, who made clear copy out of my illegibility. At an earlier time Arthur and Martha Hulings Kaemmer, both Carleton graduates, encouraged me to get on with my writing. Finally, an affectionate word for Betsy, my wife for forty-five years. Among the many good things in this relationship has been her continuing gift: to have meant it when we said, "For better, for worse . . . till death do us part." With such a companion, how could anything be all that formidable?

Northfield, Minnesota
Autumn, 1990

Introduction

My underlying question in this book is, What are the distinctive possibilities in aging? Although I believe in the continuity of lives—that all we have been through endures in memory—I am equally convinced that an important new agenda seeks to emerge in our later years. With the passage of time perspectives change. The child and young adult we once were live on within us, yet we no longer see the world or ourselves as we did at other stages. It is from these changed circumstances that aging's important new mode arises.

We cannot insist that any one of these successive outlooks is superior to the others. Life is not better at sixty than it was at sixteen; it is simply different. Especially since, as a society, we are apparently unable to affirm this fundamental fact, we need to pay attention to the extent to which we see things differently as time passes. We ignore this difference when we assess all ages by the limited enthusiasms and interests of young adults. Because they have been instructed by varied experience over the decades, older people need the opportunity to live out the understandings at which, often at considerable cost, they have arrived.

With an ever-larger group of cohorts living to ever-advanced ages, we are at the brink of a major opportunity for changing faulted social views about aging.

Resistance to my belief that our outlooks change over time comes from at least three related social attitudes: we lack any positive understanding of what it may mean to grow older; we

are ideologically wedded to but one norm for human lives (the
obligations to produce and consume); and we are antipathetic
to advanced age. We see little virtue in it, and less utility.
Absolutizing attitudes and behaviors appropriate to earlier
years of a person's life, and armed with the power of the
opinion-shaping media, we virtually force the aged to pretend
that nothing important has changed about their lives. Because
this keeps them from developments appropriate to later life, I
view such coercion as evil.

Apart from the theater, where it is reality, pretense rarely
serves a good purpose. Certainly this is true of a person's
spiritual growth: feigning is antipathetic to centering one's
life, which I believe the maturing process to be. Self-misrepre-
sentation keeps one from gathering together the multiple
strands of life in order to attend to those distinctive possibilities which inhere in longevity. The problem is, considering
society's hostility to such maturation, what is a person to do?
Since most people will sustain pretense until that becomes too
emotionally costly, the only way to get on with aging's good
work is to learn to challenge certain social attitudes.

God has a vocation for those who age. That calling begins
with learning to become part of a counterculture. Shaped by a
particular society, older people often need for their own sakes
to distance themselves from ways in which they were also
misshaped. While hardly expected, it is to be hoped that society
will gradually recognize the wisdom of this self-distancing. A
possible first step is to recognize both how ignorant and how
prejudiced against aging we really are.

None of today's varied facts about human aging is more
important to me than that there is no common positive understanding of what it means to grow old. Such agreement as
there may be is confined to prevailing negative attitudes. So
common is this negativity that we have coined the word "ageism" to identify discriminatory attitudes and practices against
the aged. The term is applied to men and women who are
unable to relate to older people without prejudice. What it
might mean positively to grow old is precisely what we do not
know and, for the most part, are reluctant to consider.

This ignorance blights the lives of increasing numbers of people. Never in human history have as many lived to an advanced age, and the prospect is for increased longevity. In that the likelihood of living beyond the biblical "threescore years and ten" applies ever more widely, an unrelieved ignorance of aging's vocation will blight us all. This threefold combination—the markedly larger generation of cohorts, ignorance about what increased longevity might mean, and the prevalence of ageism's negativities—partly accounts for what I have written. In addition to these public factors, my personal data have also influenced my thinking. An academic person in my late sixties, I am theologically educated and have served as a college chaplain for over forty years. How these various factors play into my interpretations the reader may discern more readily than I.

While I am not sure that church and synagogue have unique understandings about aging, I am convinced that they are at least as qualified as other institutions to address some of its issues. Their history and present commitment to the care of the elderly are distinctive and, in my judgment, meritorious. No single group will, I suspect, bring forth understandings to satisfy everybody. How aging may come to be understood positively is the task to which I hope diverse institutions will contribute. There are, however, several reasons that the views of the Jewish and Christian communities deserve careful consideration. They have many older members, a history as care providers, a dialectical attitude—at the same time appreciative and suspicious—toward society, and a basic rationale for interest in people at all of life's stages. Their attitude toward society and the value they attach to women and men of all ages and conditions, each as a potential means of God's self-disclosure, have contributed to my understandings.

In that I believe that the importance of the wisdom of many older people is at odds with societal ageism, I am unable to employ the sanguine imagery which has been long used to encourage people to grow old gracefully. Many have written about aging as, for example, a spiritual journey. Less irenically, I view it as a spiritual crisis. Since one's understanding of spirituality, in part, requires assent to life's "givens," an ageist atmosphere makes it unnecessarily difficult to claim one's advanced age. Since the difficulty of embracing such a natural condition arises from inimical social attitudes, a Christian spirituality requires one to challenge those views which hinder one's potential development in aging. Seeing the potential for this growth to be part of God's ordinary instruction, men and women today need most to learn to take a countercultural stand. It is this need to learn to challenge faulted social attitudes that will make aging a spiritually critical time for those previously uncritical of society. To be *in* but not *of* the world is perfect advice for those in their distinctive later years who desire to live to the glory of God.

According to my understanding of growing older, the clues about its meaning which come gradually as natural "instruction" are often ignored, if even noticed. It is impossible to age gracefully in a society that is, at the least, put off by aging's inevitability. Actually, reactions to growing old are much stronger than merely being put off. At the deepest level we may be dealing with a fear that the elderly are onto something not previously accessible. Between being put off by and becoming fearful of the aged, there is room for the host of negative feelings that empower what we have come to recognize as ageist attitudes.

Given both this reading of the social scene and my belief that God has continuing new agenda to the very end of life, I have tried to identify some of aging's new work and to suggest what will be required of those who undertake such growth. Older people's tasks are doubly difficult. At the same time as they are insisting that society provide adequately for their varied needs, they are disengaging themselves from social attitudes that would confine them to earlier stages of life. Those who find their perspectives changing with the passage of time, who want to get on with what may be God's business for their later years as distinguished from the responsibilities of earlier decades, require religion's dialectical attitude toward society. The ability to both appreciate and criticize one's community is a direct consequence of the biblical refusal to absolutize any society. Slavishness to societal convictions and prejudices will undermine the spirituality of those who lack that dialectic. For them, pretense, which is spiritually disastrous, will be the operative mode. Out of pretense comes eventually only self-disgust and fatigue, which are hardly to be mistaken for the fruits of the Spirit.

Such are some of the basic understandings I have reached over the course of at least a decade's reflection on what it might mean positively to grow old. Because I believe that it is not for nothing that God allows many so to age, I have been unable to ignore my own questions about life's meaning when earlier roles and aspirations have been largely, although always imperfectly, fulfilled. What is there after one sets aside the responsibilities and ambitions of life's earlier years? My personal question has, by virtue of changed demographics of the aging, become an urgent public issue. What can we say—beyond, "Take your leisure. You've earned it"—to an ever-larger generation of cohorts? What can we say that will not further trivialize aging?

I do not expect everybody to agree with, or even to like, my views. I fully realize that there is a down side to growing older: various illnesses may afflict us and death is assured. Neither of these, nor the loneliness often inseparable from outliving our contemporaries, is at all casual. They are realities to which we must learn to assent in the course of a maturing spirituality. Varieties of avoidance will be tried by many people. Eventually many of those who seek diversions will discover the need for a more positive approach to the fact of their own aging. It is this we must seek urgently: the ability to recognize that, with time's passage, perspectives change. We do not remain the young or middle-aged people we once were. Since such change is inescapable—I understand it as part of God's ordinary instruction—it is imperative for our maturation that we gladly embrace it. Where society tries to discourage such an embrace, we must learn to defy society. In these times the aging will be best served by becoming a counterculture.

A basic question underlies the Bible: In which of the two basic aspects of human experience, nature or history, is God most clearly and effectively present? Or, do I receive the most profound instruction about the need for change from my body or from time's passage? Scripture seems to affirm that both may be instructive. Reflecting on my own experience, it strikes me that we learn sequentially about the need for change. Initially, and perhaps finally, we learn through the experience of our bodies. Most important for my present purposes, however, time's passage is the ordinary source of tutelage in adulthood. The pedagogical importance of our lives in history arises both from the many decades in which bodily changes are minimal and from the fact that as a society, we largely ignore the instruction inherent in time's passage.

We either take seriously those new outlooks that may accompany biological changes—as in puberty or senility—or we pretend that time's passage has not influenced us. Thus, when we think at all spiritually about such matters, we confine God's means for opening our eyes to the body's infrequent, dramatic changes. This attitude is dysfunctional for two reasons. We are required to pretend contrary to our experience, and there may be decades in which our bodies provide little significant "instruction." At the time when we achieve physical maturity, when many people mistakenly assume growth to have ended, we have only reached the point when significantly different instruction may begin. Rather than biology, time becomes God's primary means of moving us toward the further stages of our evolution as persons created in the image of God. When nature's instruction diminishes dramatically, we may be brought further to our senses by the passage of time. Although nothing is assuredly instructive, God may over a long period reach us through the historical events of our lives.

The prodigal son's experiences are instructive in this regard. It was only extreme adversity that opened his eyes: when nobody would give him a scrap to eat he remembered a prior relationship he had long gladly ignored. It was in the context of starvation in an alien land that "he came to his senses" (Luke 15:17, NEB). With time's passage, perspectives may change. Of this I am utterly certain. No less important but less demonstrable is my companion belief: that such opportunity for maturation as inheres in our life in history is from God. That we have endless potential for growth and are prompted to it by time's unavoidable passage are, for me, evidence of God's gracious presence in our midst.

In a society which, at the least, inhibits people's ability to be so instructed, which encourages spiritually undermining pretenses, is there any responsible alternative to the countercultural conclusions I have reached?

This book, almost necessarily, reflects my own experience as a white, Anglo-Saxon Protestant academician and clergyman. Although I try to be sensitive to those in other groups, I cannot claim to know, much less speak for, their inner experiences. There are important books yet to be written by people within such communities.

Even so, the widespread negative attitudes to growing older afflict the majority in our society, so that any attempt to deal with these attitudes must start with the majority group.

We live with the double bind that ever-improved medical ability to extend lives is coupled with a progressive inability to honor aging's potential developments. At least three consequences of this situation matter deeply to me.

First, we withhold from the increasing numbers of aging people encouragement to get on with the appropriate tasks of the later years. With the same zeal with which we rush youth into adulthood, we insist on holding their grandparents to certain "adult" outlooks when they may desire to get free from them. Inasmuch as aging, like all of life's stages, is a combination of biological changes and societal attitudes—that is, human aging is, in part, a social construct—it is imperative that we learn to encourage maturation, now almost wholly discouraged in America. Put simply, we need to learn to recognize the beauty and challenge inherent in growing older.

The second consequence of the largely ignored double bind can be put simply. Inasmuch as society's discouragements are effective, we drive people to pretend to be other than they are. Although some pretense is probably inescapable in life, such deception—often more convincing to the deceiver than to oth-

ers—can never be the basis of a mature spirituality. Falsehood
cannot yield liberating truth.

The third consequence of the double bind is that it blinds us
to God's enabling presence in the issues of life's later stages.
In large part because of the misidentification of evidences of
that Presence in adulthood's earlier decades—for example,
that the ability to work hard to succeed is a key evidence of
grace instead of the workaholism it really is—many are immobilized. Whatever should be happening as life winds down
fails to intrigue those who remain unrewardingly trapped in
the pursuit of success, the cultivation of appearance, and
concentration on externals.

Two fundamental assumptions undergird my approach.
First, for theological reasons I am convinced that life's last
years hold no less potential evidence of God's blessing than
many earlier stages. This belief is basic to my argument.
However mixed is the blessing of aging, with its positive and
negative aspects, it is vital that the aging process not be viewed
primarily as either a bad joke or a curse. The second assumption is that my prospective readers are mainline Christians,
often privileged, who have begun to experience some disillusionment with the values underlying adulthood's pursuits.
Given the ubiquity and power of prevailing middle-class aspirations, how can the privileged be helped to recognize and take
seriously promptings, which I believe to be from God, to reconsider "adulthood's" inability to value much other than production and consumption and the competitive spirit that maxi-
mizes both?

Observing how the aged cope in other and quite different
contexts—the worldwide evidence is wonderfully diverse—will
do little to move the privileged toward such reconsideration.
Evidence of successful aging by those in other cultures, or of
the ways of coping by those at the margins of our own culture,
will not provide the motivation I believe to be required. We
must challenge the ageism by which ever greater numbers of
men and women are being held back from inner developments
of public significance in which God's continued presence may
be recognized. Indeed, one of the effects of judging negatively

all of the diverse ingredients in the extended process of aging is the inability to recognize and appreciate the varied ways in which people grow old in different social settings.

As an aging, privileged Christian, I want to be liberated for those developments to which society assigns such little value. Strong individuals may encourage me to get on with whatever "nonsense" I claim to be God's agenda for life's later years. As a Christian, however, I may not be satisfied with a wholly private solution to these issues. Because the conflicting pressures are both societal and personal, the former seeking to confine or contain needs for maturation which come with time's passage, there is no effective resolution purely within individuals. We have before us an issue of social ethics.

Mere encouragement to exercise will power to be different, which may indeed be preferable to denying that time's passage makes for change, overlooks the power of social attitudes. Much more than we ordinarily recognize, all people are deeply imbued with enthusiasm for those aspects of the human potential which a society encourages. Whether or not, for example, competitiveness is really more basic than our ability to cooperate need not be demonstrable to be widely believed. Such preferences for certain aspects of the human "arc," to use a term that Ruth Benedict introduced earlier in this century, gives each society its distinctive dynamic. However, determining how to combine competitiveness and cooperation in a society that prefers one over the other is a less difficult undertaking than dealing with the attitudes that discourage people from getting on with tasks appropriate to life's later years. If one lives, and the "medicalization" of aging tends to encourage longevity, there is nowhere to go other than into old age. To date, Ponce de Leon's successors have been no more successful than he in the search for the springs of eternal youth. Any Oil of Olay is at best an unguent of delay. Indefinite postponement of growing old eludes us.

In that aging cannot be denied, how, other than with repugnance, are we to react when that which occurs inevitably is not gladly embraced? What, other than anger, is an appropriate response to the need to deny and suppress those possible maturations of later life because they may be somewhat at odds with adulthood's prevailing values? In this book I try to draw upon the energy inherent in these emotions of anger and repugnance to fashion means by which those most committed to adulthood's values, with their consequent ageism, may be freed to recognize the emergence in their later years of other, not always complementary, values. As in racism for those who cannot change their color, and sexism, so I see in ageism the scourge to be felt by all who continue to live. For me, there is never a warrant for negative attitudes toward those things which are unchangeable. Only a pathological society thinks otherwise. Witness, as a worst case, the ovens of the Holocaust.

It is as one shaped by adulthood's values, from which I yearn in a measure to be liberated, that I have written about aging. I am convinced of the imperative to modify the present stasis. We must unfreeze the attitudes in which youth are trained, and to which many adults give themselves with varying effectiveness, that issue in the most diminished opportunities for the aging. What prospects there are for encouraging men and women to become critics of attitudes and practices that eventually demean them, I do not know. I am not sanguine on this score. Believing as I do, however, that the privilege of aging is one of God's benefactions rather than a cruel joke, I have no alternative to writing about the costs and rewards of a countercultural vocation in one's later years.

Although the inherent problems are not amenable to merely individual solutions, the fact is that by the very process of time's passage, God will open the eyes of some who had been uncritically committed to adulthood's values. By such subtle means does God work against societal ideology. Among those so illumined, or de-illusioned, some will work imaginatively and persistently to modify ageism's dominance of popular attitudes. Taking up such a later-life vocation, they will become spokespersons for the long-lost age in which all stages through which persons might pass were honored as ingredients of their God-given potential for wholeness. Or, perhaps, they will model for others a future in which human creation in the image of God will everywhere be celebrated. For those for whom such eschatological visioning is excessive, we may say more moderately that what is needed minimally is an enlargement of the range of positive human experience to which encouragement is given. Of all the points at which such enlargement is overdue, surely people's later years must have high priority. In due time such enlargement will bless all lives by encouraging endless maturation. So liberated, some will recognize what have been largely unrecognizable evidences of the nurturing grace of God over the entire spectrum, cradle to grave.

Chapter 1
Spirituality in Aging: Regaining One's Balance

Not long ago I wrote a book that emphasized the new learning potential in growing old.[1] Although I believe that thesis is still valid, I have come to recognize the insufficiency of the reasonable approach there employed. Indirectness will not begin to dismantle society's arsenal of negative myths about aging. Until we expose the harmfulness of these views, there is no hope of encouraging people to undertake somewhat gladly what aging's good work may be. Such hope will be grounded in the realization that a countercultural stance is most promising for the aging. Popular social attitudes undermine that hope. What we need is an orientation that will enable men and women, against considerable contrary social pressure, to pay attention to the instruction inherent in their accumulated experience. We must not allow society to determine our understanding of what aging means.

Given both scholarly uncertainty about the means or the meaning of mass aging and the unsympathetic societal attitudes toward growing old, we must include ageism with racism and sexism as negative attitudes that keep people from seeking their appropriate fulfillment. *Those who have positive convictions about what growing old might mean must add their voices to the increasing public discussion of this crucial topic.* Markedly increased longevity has made imperative greater clarity about these issues. When those who lived beyond seventy years were but a small minority of the population, it was possible

25

largely to ignore these concerns. Such benign neglect has now
become intolerable. Unless they are willing to let society define
what aging means, which prospect I abhor, religious institutions must fashion, voice, and defend what may be their distinctive understandings of what growing older means.

Thus, if we want to view aging's work positively in the face
of negative popular opinion, we must think of our later years
as a stage of life when, in order to attend to emerging new
agenda, we have to become capable of standing *against* the
culture. Almost a decade after a reasonably successful book on
mid-life,[2] I found myself wondering again about the adequacy
of a society that valued absolutely only a very limited aspect
of total human experience. When I began to try to identify the
changes occurring in the seventh decade of my own life, I found
myself bumping repeatedly into narrow but dominating societal enthusiasms for production and consumption which seemed
decreasingly relevant to my experience. Familiar stimuli of the
commercial world failed to arouse me. Certain social attitudes
now seem hostile to the emerging interests of my own later
years. There are considerations other than economic profitability and national defense, and it may be that older people will
be responsible for disclosing and defending them. There are
means other than the extremes of contemporary competitiveness by which *human* life may be evoked. Thus, what began as
a comparatively innocent effort to understand my own *changing* experience on the edge of retirement has turned into a
confrontation with the society by which I have been shaped
and misshaped. Especially in view of the increasing numbers
of people who will live long, it is imperative that we clear away
our misunderstandings of life's last stage.

The point that cannot be overemphasized is that in approaching the subject of aging—and all else, actually—*the
context is decisive for the outcome to be determined.* We see only
what the environment in which we look permits us to recognize. Since this entire book elaborates my conviction about the
decisiveness of one's avenue of approach, let me suggest briefly
some of the ingredients of the countercultural context I am
advancing. First, I am convinced that we may never approach

human aging as merely a natural phenomenon. Although human beings are part of the organic world in which all things grow old and eventually die, there is always more to a human life than its kinship with the world of nature. For a host of reasons to be adduced below, humans do not relate to time's passage as do the creatures and organisms around us. It is because of human *self*-consciousness that our aging is never just natural: we cannot simply equate ourselves with things in nature. This recognition is the source of the imperative I feel to resist all efforts so to reduce the elderly! We will grow old and die as do all flora and fauna; however, no human will die as they do.

Second, our approach to aging will be countercultural because the values operative in life's middle decades are not only too narrow to serve all age groups but also *just too serious*. It may seem that I am but substituting one seriousness for another. To an extent that is true. Ideally, as Shakespeare often did (which may have been the key to his enduring appeal), we must be able to affirm both tragedy and comedy. Life is never for long just one or the other. The undertaker becomes a comic character, or a source of comedy, because he overburdens the reality of loss; the great clowns take us through amusement to the tears beyond laughter. In the Bard's plays there is seriousness within the comedies and, even more noticeably, comic scenes within the tragedies. Who but a genius would have introduced clowns-as-grave-diggers at that point in *Hamlet* (5.1) at which the final stage is set for massive bloodletting? In most instances Shakespeare appropriately incorporated tragic and comic elements. His theater mirrored life—or suggested a way of coming at life without being either trivialized or overwhelmed.

Not so, I find, in his attitude toward aging. In that he was prisoner to his own times and/or to his personal health. The premature death of his son at age eleven and the premonition of his own demise at age fifty-two may have over instructed him. What I believe to be aging's potential for reviving the long-suppressed comic approach to life is precisely what is utterly lacking in Shakespeare's characterizations of old age.

"Despairing" is the word that comes to mind when I think of
his words about life's final years, which he gives to Jacques in
the Forest of Arden:

> . . . the sixth age shifts
> Into the lean and slippered pantaloon,
> With spectacles on nose and pouch on side;
> His youthful hose, well saved, a world too wide
> For his shrunk shank, and his big manly voice,
> Turning again toward childish treble, pipes
> And whistles in his sound. Last scene of all,
> That ends this strange eventful history,
> Is second childishness and mere oblivion,
> Sans teeth, sans eyes, sans taste, sans everything.[3]

Here is no tragicomic blend. In a uniformly cynical characterization of life's seven ages, the last stages are seen as pure
loss. Because of the inevitable physical diminution, it is even a
mistake to try to save clothing for one's old age. I was long
immobilized by the writer's utterly bleak characterization of
the "last scene of all." "Second childishness and mere oblivion"
are hardly attractive alternatives to the strengths and ambitions of adulthood's decades. Shakespeare will not help us in
this matter. The regrettable fact, which is our primary challenge, is that many of our contemporaries reflect his bleak
outlook on aging. Evidence to the contrary notwithstanding,
current opinion often views aging as "sans everything."

We have no alternative but to lament the writer's lack of
genius on this subject. Great as he was, I do not find in his
plays the basis for affirming both the losses and the gains
inherent in growing older. That there are gains is, I believe,
undeniable; that one will have to proceed against the societal
grain in order to enjoy them is no less the case. What Shakespeare was unable to recognize in the late sixteenth century,
and has hardly been a dominant theme since then, we have the
need and opportunity to actualize in the late twentieth.

Like Shakespeare at his best, what we propose about aging
will hold together the tragic and the comic. Clearly, growing
older involves both losses and gains. That this combination has

been true over the earlier decades, in which people often pretend there is nothing but gain, is an awareness for which one may fondly hope. Meanwhile, for the sake of all those able to acknowledge that they are aging, there are positive gains to recognize and celebrate. To further such celebration I argue our need to make aging a counterculture.

The prevailing culture is faulted as Shakespeare was in his attitude toward aging: it sees appreciatively too little of the human spectrum. In a context defined by those in the productive and reproductive decades, no provision is made for others who are either not yet or no longer enamored of certain consumerist criteria. This inability to encourage other than the most limited aspects of growth—the accumulative—is unwarrantedly punitive to the aged and must be challenged. However undervalued by a misguided society life's later decades may be, there is important and somewhat distinctive growth inherent in them. It is this growth we seek to identify in the following chapters and, however antipathetic it may be to prevailing attitudes, to encourage older people to take up.

THE TASKS OF LIFE'S LATER YEARS

Since I reject the prevailing ideas of what aging means, I want to contribute to the efforts to identify positive human tasks appropriate to life's later years. The current demographic facts are unique to our time. A large percentage of people are living, often in good health, well beyond the biblical threescore and ten. Considering these statistics and the variety of positive understandings available to offset society's ageist attitudes, representatives of religious communities have an opportunity to suggest agenda for older people that arise from their varied traditions. It is in this capacity that I propose the understandings to which I have come. They are not the last word. There may never be such. Provisional understandings may be the best of which we are capable; they may also reflect the variety of perspectives in an increasingly pluralistic society. The point I must emphasize is that we need to move far beyond society's narrow and negative understanding of what it means to grow old. As long as these current views prevail, people will be socialized on faulty assumptions and will try to conform their later years to what they have been told aging means. What they should be breaking away from in the name of greater wholeness, they will—at the cost of even greater pretense—attempt to embody. Only inauthenticity and its attendant frustrations will result.

Given the foreseeable numbers of men and women who will be living to quite advanced ages in the decades immediately ahead, and given the misguided popular attitudes toward and fear of aging, the prevailing ageism will not serve the needs of this ever-increasing group of people. One hopes they will not tolerate attitudes that were never adequate but were endured because the tide of human resistance was too weak to wash them away. That situation has changed. The tide will continue to rise for an indefinite time. Much attitudinal debris will yield reluctantly to the new forces. From my own Christian perspective I want to contribute to the ongoing discussion of what, in these times, it may mean to grow old. Although I may be unable to identify God's intent for life's later years even to my own satisfaction, I do not believe that it is for nothing that many of us will live longer than did most of our predecessors.

It has become increasingly clear that we may be instructed about these matters by the very passage of time we take so for granted. In my attempts to identify what the experience of aging may mean I shall pay careful attention to the directions in which, involuntarily, we find ourselves moving. That which satisfies or stimulates at an early stage will rarely persist for a lifetime. Yet such changes may provide useful clues as to where we might like to be headed in those decades beyond the middle years. It is quite conceivable to me that, even in a society with an unconscionable number of mindless diversions, long-entertained (and bored) men and women may, without willing anything to be different, find their hearts restless for pursuits other than the trivial. Spirituality in aging may depend on the ineradicable image of God in which we all are made. The *imago dei* will not forever tolerate its trivialization.

Is it possible that part of aging's work might be viewed as the recovery of that playfulness lost too early in childhood and

effectively buried in purposeful adulthood? Whereas playfulness might include the occasional game, the term is used to
refer to an utterly different dimension of human experience. It
may help us to recover the wholeness, or potential for it, that
we once had. Inasmuch as indifference to the need to be in
control is central to what I mean by the spirit of play, it may
be seen as a complement to midlife's rigorous intentionality.
To urge as aging's spiritual work the reclamation of the ability
for merriment is not to advocate indifference to social injus-
tices. Rather, in a society lopsidedly tipped to seriousness on
the assumption that everything depends on us, I seek in aging
a balance between initiative and resignation, between tragedy
and comedy.

Spokespersons for religion may resent as "unworthy" the
suggestion that the recovery of the capacity for play may be
intrinsic to God's intent for the long-lived. Is the capacity for
play inherent to Christian spirituality? On the assumption
that the final assignment, religious or otherwise, is to yield up
one's life somewhat gracefully, is it not the case that much
must be recovered before it can be relinquished? In her extremely stimulating journal, Florida Scott-Maxwell, in her
eighties, ventures this question: "When at last age has assembled you together, will it not be easy to let it all go, lived,
balanced over?"[4] Those who may be less sanguine than she is
about letting go of one's life, for example, those who resonate
more readily with the order of Dylan Thomas to "go not gentle
into that good night," may be relieved to discover the sentences
that immediately precede her seemingly glib question. In the
context of an assertion that all one must do to become oneself
is to claim the events of one's life, she insists: "When you truly
possess all you have been and done, which may take some time,
you are fierce with reality."[5] Originally electrified by these
visions, I am now most impressed by her acknowledgement
that the process of self-reclamation will "take some time."

Older people, however urgent the need, will not quickly
regain their long-lost ability to play. The more I think of what
we seem determined to do to children to assure them a competitive edge, the more vividly do paintings come to mind from an

era before childhood had any distinctive value. In the Renaissance and into the Baroque Age, little boys and girls were
dressed identically to their parents; children were but minia-
turized adults. Between then and now we have learned more.
Childhood, which has little to do with Shakespeare's "second
childishness," is a precious stage of life from which gains
should be carried forward to flavor the next decades. However,
as a society, we little appreciate childhood's qualities, especially its playfulness, and seem committed to moving boys and
girls as early and as far away from it as possible. The consequences of this, for what may be among the developments of
later life, range from awkwardness to inhibition. Whatever
Jesus might have meant by suggesting that God's kingdom
yielded only to the "assault" of little children, it is clear that
most of us will have none of that nonsense.

While my proposal may be accused of trivializing both aging
and spirituality, I urge it as an antidote to the illusions of
control which inform so much adult effort. That every human
attribute has its necessary and desirable complement is a basic
truth of which we have lost sight. The need to be in control
must be balanced by acknowledgement of the impossibility of
total control in any significant area of experience. The ability
to affirm such ambivalences, which run throughout all lives
always, is for me both what Christian faith makes possible and
what aging is about. *It is by that faith that one knows how to be*
responsible without ever fully controlling; it will be in aging
understood as requiring a countercultural stance that we may
be helped to recover the God-given balance of our lives. As well
as benefiting older people directly, enabling them to get about
business appropriate to their stage of life, regaining one's
balance serves a larger social purpose. The person recovering
from adulthood's imbalances is responsible to witness to the
wisdom of the reclaimed wholeness. Although it is partly for
themselves that the aged will pursue their vocation, the em-
bodiment of that new life is also for the liberation of those
younger persons unwillingly trapped in adulthood's narrow
purposefulness. We were created for more than intentionality.
Is it too much to suggest that as we age, God calls us back to

the "something more" by the insufficiency of our field of concentration? In our awareness of how much more there is to our
lives than the society takes seriously, are we not lured forward
to a vocation commensurate with both our needs and our
experience-derived capabilities? Over the course of time needs
change as ability mounts.

Although some observable biological changes accompany the
years in which we grow older, we rarely ask whether such
involuntary modifications suggest aging's distinctive work. My
assumptions about life's ordinary instructions preclude assigning any lesson exclusively to one of life's stages, yet some
things are learned more readily at one time than another.
Thus, whatever aging cohorts grasp somewhat easily may be
accessible to younger people but is rarely pursued by them.[6]
Apart from lessons about health maintenance in the interest
of longevity, which too many people assume to be the only
positive instruction amid scores of negative reminders, *biological aging does not provide a clue as to what may be aging's
possibly distinctive developments and consequent service to the
society.* (Whereas gerontologists give thought to maturations
associated with later life, to my knowledge nobody sees older
people as an informed source of social criticism. Our understanding of the services within their capability is largely
limited to one-on-one care.) Biological reminders of the fact
that I am growing older may encourage efforts at fitness; they
do not in themselves remind me of my kinship with other men,
women and children. Lacking that sense of connectedness I
may remain indifferent to their health. At any age I may
pursue personal wellness in as self-isolating ways and for as
selfish reasons as people do many things. My question is this:
Is there alternative instruction with which aging may acquaint
us? If so, and in the interest of societal well-being, it is
important to recognize it.

Since those things most easily associated with aging are
largely noninstructive about whatever may be aging's business, and since prevailing attitudes diminish both elderly
people and what society might learn from then, I propose that
it is imperative to try to change social attitudes. The possibility

of liberation from merely negative feelings about growing older requires identification of important tasks for the aged which will be both within their capability and of potential social benefit. Apart from the churches and synagogues which, often without knowing *why* they do it, insist on the sacredness and interrelatedness of lives at all their stages, no other agencies are likely to be interested in the task. As a member of one such community I propose that affirming aging as counterculture is a way to identify the relevant and demanding work that the aging virtually alone are able to do. Willingness to undertake this task may be influenced by the realization that the very *process* of aging is one's primary equipment for the work.

THE UNIQUE TASK OF AGING

The task of witness is twofold: to begin to reclaim something of one's largely neglected personal life and, in conjunction with that reclamation, to recall the social changes that have occurred over one's lifetime. These assignments acknowledge the importance of both the personal and public dimensions of lives and assume their interdependence. As mentioned at the outset, public *attitudes* can either hinder, as in our case, or assist men and women to come to terms with aging's inevitability and possible opportunities. As they discover themselves to belong to a counterculture, an awareness that often occurs at or about the time of retirement, the aged may both help themselves by better self-acquaintance and make their somewhat distinctive contribution to those who are younger by reminding them of the transience of present social arrangements which are so easily absolutized. It will be a loving work of recollection and social criticism.

My agenda for the elderly may not be to everybody's liking. It has, however, at least two virtues: in a society which at best trivializes the process of growing older, I take extended memory—both individual and public—seriously, and believe that the varied work of personal reclamation is within everybody's capability. The findings will not be identical, nor will the work be easy; the society has not encouraged reflection. In the process of reclaiming their lives and lifetimes, and gradually recognizing the inseparability of inwardness and the external world, many will be engaged for the first time appropriately in the search for God's presence. In my understanding the work is spiritual because the aged witness seeks in love to reconnect with his or her own life as it has unfolded in particular times and places. Through awareness of that history, which influences our life much more than we realized as it happened, we connect both with our own cohorts and with those shaped by later circumstances. When we are preoccupied with the recovery of our life and with recognizing the fate of others we are, I believe, in the presence of that God for whom love inheres in love for the neighbor as for self. Jesus' summary of Jewish Law is predicated on the inseparability of the components of the life-giving triad: God-neighbor-self.[7] It will only be as we connect, or reconnect, with both our personal life and our lifetime—the distinctive circumstances through which we have lived—that we may discover our later-life vocation as witnesses. For it will be in the painfully rewarding process of reacquaintance with what was happening within and around us that we open ourselves to possible awareness of God's presence. All who have lived through them may recognize that momentous things have gone on in recent decades; some of us may realize that these events shaped our lives much more than we acknowledged. Only a handful of men and women will make the life-giving discovery that it is precisely at the juncture of the public and the personal that God is to be encountered. God begins to become God for us only as we undertake to assume responsibility for both our personal lives and the social circumstances in which those lives unfolded. Not all will be eager for this work of reclamation. Some will be forever blinded to the process by which they may discover that vocation, and to the work itself. Others may have their eyes opened to the desirability of becoming an elderly witness but will be unwilling to imperil the rewards that society has for those who go along quietly. Still others, who see and affirm aging's possibly distinctive work, will find cohorts willing to share the load, and together they will find effective ways of witnessing to

what they have discovered about themselves and the world of
their times.

Without abandoning their personal lives they will realize
gladly how much like all other people they are; without losing
sight of the patterned social fabric into which their life threads
were woven they will continue to affirm the irreducibility of
their individual lives. Having grasped these basic dimensions
of human experience—the individual self and others, each of
whom long pretends an unwarranted independence of the
other—such elders will be strong in ways rare to and much
needed in our society. With such strength the aged will resist
further trivialization, and they will be bold to expose the
extent to which life is both diminished and imperiled by a
commercialized, ever more homogenized society. Profitability
is too narrow a criterion for the maintenance and enhancement
of human lives. What has been done to the environment in the
past half century is not only the most obvious but probably the
most ominous evidence that somebody needs to challenge prevailing values. Is not this a God-given paradox: that it is
precisely *because* they are closer to death that elder witnesses
find intolerable our apparent willingness to let the world
become uninhabitable? Is it not ironically instructive that the
fate of the future, if there is to be one, may depend on those
with deep memories rather than those preoccupied with only
the present?

That many of those who are uncritical of such absolutes as
profitability will not like what aging witnesses may have to
say will, according to Cicero, be nothing new. In one of the
great essays on aging, written over two millennia ago, the
Roman orator reported an exchange between Pisastratus and
Solon in consequence of a takeover of Athens, to which the
latter took exception: "When the tyrant demanded of Solon
how he durst be so bold, or wherein he reposed his trust . . .
Solon answered him that he trusted to his old age, and that
was it that made him full of courage . . . forasmuch as he . . .
had attempted to suppress the commonwealth."[8] These ancient
words underscore two vital questions: Who, other than the
elderly, are capable of such concern for future human well-

being? What is it about being older that equips some for such witness?

We shall speak to both of these questions; however, it may be helpful to recognize first some of the major features of advancing age which, somewhat uniquely, equip people for later life's vocation. At least two factors move them in what I claim to be the complementary directions of progressive detachment from their own lives and progressive attachment to the history of their times. First, although younger people have no less need to be aware of their mortality, for the most part it is the aged who must most urgently come to terms with the prospect of death. As the existentialists soundly insist, by embracing this fact one takes life *more seriously* than is otherwise possible. We must not be put off by this paradox. Second, the aged have a different perspective because they are less involved in the prevailing socioeconomic system to which they once gave themselves. Vastly less swayed by its lures and rewards, elder witnesses are capable of recognizing the flaws in attitudes and practices they may once have defended vigorously. Because they are human inventions and tend always to serve certain interests more than others, all systems need such informed and loving criticism. Happily, there is evidence that some of the staunchest defenders of the business and military status quo become equally persuasive voices of social conscience when they leave the system.

One such transition was experienced by a man who served more than a decade on the Carleton College Board of Trustees and for a time was its chairperson. During these years he was the CEO of Honeywell, Inc., and an articulate defender of the company's responsibility to help meet his country's needs for arms. In these roles Edson Spencer was not distinguishable from the other able people who chaired America's top corporations and colleges.

But a newspaper headline, "Spencer's Views Shift as He Goes to Ford Foundation,"[9] and accompanying article illustrate my contention that the emergence of a heartening social conscience may depend upon a person's withdrawal from the socioeconomic system: "As Chairman of the Ford Foundation . . .

[Spencer] hopes for a decrease in U.S. arms production so that
the government can turn to the needs of single-parent families,
homeless people, and the rural poor." Since he did not articulate such views before his career change, despite extended
membership on the Ford Foundation board, he would appear to
have been freed to voice socially creative views by stepping out
of the corporate system.

It is apparently not possible to be simultaneously in and out
of any system. The potential for new and radical understandings is possible for those who, having been within, *are now
somewhat beyond the system.* Caught up as most of us are in a
system with its own distinctive strengths and weaknesses, we
have little possibility short of life's later years of recognizing
either the futility of many of our undertakings or the damage
done to our sensibilities in their pursuit. Not many of those
still within any system will be able to hear words from those
outside of it, even when the latter are informedly loving. Some,
however, will be helped to recognize present perils and to
consider alternative courses when addressed by those who have
experience within the system on which they have reflected.
Reflective evaluation may be a way to describe the contribution
of elders like Edson Spencer, who are somewhat uniquely
capable in their post-career vocation.

CHANGING FOCUS FROM SELF TO SOCIETY

Growing older means both a gradual detachment from one's
individual life and a complementary deepening attachment to
the public events of one's lifetime. (This does not mean the
abandonment of one's life. Neither suicide nor gross personal
neglect is commendable. Rather, in a society that has lost all
nuanced sense of the importance of an individual life, it is
inevitable that extended experience will suggest for some a
gradual withdrawal from an unwarranted emphasis on individual uniqueness and importance.) This combination involves,
on one hand, a growing appreciation for how much like others
one is and, on the other, an increasing awareness of the
influence of external events on one's life. Progressive recognition of the inseparability of these inner and outer worlds and

the appreciation for both as fundamental components of one's identity, are among God's most important gifts in life's later years. Although awareness of this complementarity is theoretically possible in earlier decades, the tendencies then are to be preoccupied with one or the other, either individuality, which is the West's precious illusion, or the East's penchant for stressing the group's needs. From such distorting overemphasis on either self or society some people find corrective instruction in the process of aging. For such instructive reminders of the inseparability of self and others I credit God's working through time's passage to modify the faulted perspectives of earlier decades. It may just be impossible in one's earlier years to avoid any of a number of imbalanced emphases, for example, one's individual distinctiveness as against one's likeness to and kinship with others, one's ability to be in control as against many unchangeable factors, the endless capacity for initiative as against the need for acceptance of (even resignation to) unforeseen obstacles, the pursuit of success as against all other considerations, the uniform preference for action over contemplation. The fact is that young and middle life achieves its distinctive power by selective attention/inattention rather than by the comprehensiveness of its interests.

With the passage of time many people find themselves thinking about both the insufficiency of their particular overemphases and some of the neglected ingredients of their particular lives. The former have a way of becoming tiresome, or at least tiring. The latter, which arise from our givenness, seek acknowledgement. Often these interior movements are "explained" by boredom and the need for novelty. Yet God may often work through our boredoms and those long-neglected aspects of our being. The effort to concern ourselves with only some fragment of reality is, in time, bound to bore us, because it is a lie to pretend that any part is equal to the whole. There is much more to the world than any particular concentration *and* there is both the ability and the need to relate to ever more of that comprehensiveness. Pretense does not indefinitely sustain. Similarly, there is always more to each of us than whatever we may have pretended was the whole person. Under-

valued and long neglected, these facets of our being need to be
acknowledged by us and by others. We have resources deeper
than is suggested by our traditional self-presentation. Again,
pretense is not indefinitely adequate. Both out there in the
world and in the inner person there really is more truth to
embrace. To concentrate indefinitely on a part of anything as
though it were the whole is to assure undernourishment. A
part will not suffice.

The gradually recognized yearning for wholeness that characterizes life's later years is one of God's gifts. We were not
created for selective indifference to aspects of our genetic
equipment or of our time and place of birth. Both of these will
make our individual journeys toward wholeness somewhat
different in detail. Beneath all such uniqueness, however, we
all need to recognize the folly of our early efforts to substitute
a part for the whole. Something, or someone, will have to
remind us of the good news: we are always more than we
pretend.

Such instruction surely tries to get through to us in our later
years. Depending on its success, we either cling ever more
desperately to our illusions of utter distinctiveness or, without
ever abandoning our selfhood, begin to detach from our unwarranted self-importance and uniqueness. We are aided in that
detachment process by the gradual realization that the cost of
maintaining pretenses about how different we are outweighs
the benefits. Fatigue is often quite instructive. Is it not the
case that truthfulness is valued in part because it is less
fatiguing? Depending again on the success of that later-life
instruction, either we become progressively indifferent to and
seemingly isolated from the history through which we have
lived or, without trying to avoid responsibility for the shape of
our lives, we recognize ever more clearly the impact that
certain public events of our time have had on us. In this positive
process of life's later years men and women become capable of
the crucial, interrelated work of reclaiming both their lives
and their lifetimes. That both activities are important and
inescapably interrelated is what empowers the witness of articulate older people. Being in touch with their own experience

gives them a rare degree of authority. In many instances they have seen it all and have still avoided cynicism. But it is not just their personal, inner experience with which they are familiar. Mere nostalgia is not the resource I have in mind. They know also something of the power of some of the major public events of their lifetime. Thus their witness is neither just autobiographically private nor mere institutional history. The witness we seek is neither as steamy as the one nor as sterile as the other. It will be the corrective witness of those who have lived long enough to have moved beyond the de-illusionment of their middle years and become able to acknowledge the pathos of many of the absolutes to which they unconditionally gave themselves.

This is a vocation for the later years which at least has the virtue of being anything but trivial. The process of reclaiming a long-neglected life with but a minimum of distortion will take the best efforts of most people. To get at such reclamations older people may have to create means to tell their stories to each other. These dynamics are worlds away from the clever stories by which some long amused others.

Further, to see one's life less as an isolated private entity than as a part of some larger social entity is challenging at several levels. Most obviously, it requires us to move beyond the illusions of an absolute individualism, in which many are well instructed, without losing contact with the life one lived. Beyond that—and the work does not get easier—we will struggle to recall both major public events of our time and their impact on our thoughts and feelings. Why did many massive happenings have little or no impact on our sensibilities? Whereas there may be millions of white Americans who recall little more about the civil rights movement than Bull Connor's dogs and fire hoses, the lives of millions of others, black and white, would never be the same because of these events. This work of personal/public recall and witness may not satisfy the voyeuristic interests of readers of the people-oriented magazines; rather it will speak to the pilgrimage-interests of those who care about the future of a world careening toward disaster. Rather than sedating their hearers with an abstract history, the senior witnesses I have in mind will invigorate inquirers, because the public events about which they will write and speak have been embodied in their personal experience. The mushroom cloud in the New Mexico desert, soon thereafter to appear over two Japanese cities, was not only a social fact. It was, as J. Robert Oppenheimer tried to say, the end of at least one world.

In addition to its nontriviality, this radical vocation is theoretically *open to all* aging persons. The credentials for participation are within the capability of any person whose memory is somewhat intact; the only requirement is the willingness to dig persistently into the past for the sake of the present and the future. It will be a work that takes seriously the transformative capabilities of millions of older men and women whom the society has every inclination to trivialize. Perhaps I am too sanguine about what is possible. That older people become competent fighters for their own needs, following the impressive leads of the Gray Panthers and the American Association of Retired Persons (AARP), may be enough to hope for in these times. In so far as their efforts ignore what is happening to the society, however, their selfishness will not be sustainable and they will engender serious intergenerational conflict. It is imperative to demonstrate that one's witness arises from the desire to enhance society's present and future well-being. That such desire arises from the process of getting back in touch with the past may also suggest to others the need for less frenzied, more reflective lives.

Just as society needs the corrective witness of countercultural elders, those older people need a compelling sense of radical vocation for their later years. As all life is indebted from the outset to the society into which it was born, this vocation-as-witness, which I believe is from God, is a way for a grateful critic to acknowledge that continuing interdependence.

Here again we confront the inseparability of individual and social life. As they age, persons have the need to assemble their life experiences meaningfully. Although the ultimate purpose of such reclamation is to enable one to let go of that life gracefully, the possibility of such crucial work presupposes a society gradually able to allow people to grow old. Rather than a society with narrow emphases that require older people to ignore their distinctive business, to pretend interests they may well have lost, I envision a society able to value the changing enthusiasms and preoccupations of a lifetime.

It is as an expression of that supportive relationship and out of a desire to discourage its further deterioration that I have urged the aged to learn a countercultural stance. It is precisely that relationship which is imperiled by contemporary negative attitudes toward aging. Ultimately, it is the *imago dei* that present arrangements threaten. Could the challenge be more serious?

Chapter 2

Experience and Faith

In this chapter I want to identify in general terms the issues with which we are fundamentally concerned throughout the book. As the title suggests, "Experience *and* Faith," it is the content of these categories and, especially, their relationship that interest me. We are familiar with Paul Tillich's discussion in which experience poses questions and challenges the adequacy of prior faith-formations; however, I shall argue for a genuinely two-way relationship. Indeed, although I recognize gladly the ways in which experience may encourage faith's maturation, I also suspect that most of us restrain our God-given potential for experience because of the shallowness of our faith. The extent of experience that we are able to affirm is as dependent on our faith as is our faith challenged by our experience. The interdependence is unending. It is tempting to assign the greater importance to one or the other; perhaps over the course of a lifetime the valuation changes several times. It is my intention, however artificial the effort, to hold these two dimensions of our lives in tension with each other. Whether or not the effort will prove productive or even possible we shall see anon.

FAITH LIMITS EXPERIENCE

Experience may as easily be restricted as enlarged; it does not necessarily tend to expand, as we are often led to assume. How much experience a person may claim or acknowledge as potential depends on the adequacy of that person's faith. Each

45

of us has an outlook on the world, some basic convictions about
what is true, and these necessarily set limits for us as to what
is and what is not. Our beliefs are that important. Our convictions actually both enable us to see and limit the amount of
reality we can see. The point to be clear about, as the Bible
reiterates, is that sight—and hearing, for that matter—is not
a natural ability. We do not take in everything, we see and
hear selectively. The key to one's selectivity is the faith affirmed. Rarely are these realities as clearly set forth as in the
1987 parliamentary elections in the United Kingdom. Note the
dissimilar ideologies, assumptions about what is really true
about the world, of the Labour and Conservative candidates
for the office of prime minister, according to one reporter:

> What [Neil] Kinnock sees in the British people is a sense
> of community, of fairness, of sharing, of creativity. . . . He
> offers as his own conviction the belief that personal profit
> is not the only form of human motivation, nor the free
> market the only form of efficient society. . . . But Mrs.
> Thatcher . . . believes to the uttermost reaches of her being
> that the human instinct is, above all, to get on, make
> money, look after number one, find its sense of community
> in the aggregation of individual success. Society should be
> organized to that individualistic end.[1]

Although this reporter's description of the extremes offered
to British voters may have been artificially clear, I had the
sense, from reasonably close observation during the campaign
weeks, that he had not seriously misrepresented the candidates. Inasmuch as his descriptions are accurate, we have
comparatively rare straightforward public evidence of how
fundamental convictions make it possible to see certain things
clearly and impossible to see other things at all. Just as the
Labour candidate is unable to acknowledge self-interest as the
fundamental human motivation, so the Conservative cannot
see the rudimentary reality to which the opposition points—
the sense of community, fairness, sharing. We may be tempted
to dismiss these differences as merely political. Some skepticism about such matters is probably healthy, but it does not

serve us if it blinds us to the reality of such convictions and of their power to influence, if not to determine, what we can and cannot see. The realities with which we are immediately concerned are not limited to politics. Different basic convictions surely underlie the dissimilar ranges of experiences emphasized in the African and European communities. The importance of the women's movement to both women and men has its source in just such differing convictions. Male and female experiences are probably somewhat unlike at all points as, I increasingly suspect, are the differences between youth's and age's experiences of the same event.

Polarizing realities are currently at work in many parts of the world. Such beautiful hopes as modern democratic liberalism had for the increasing sway of a detached reason in human affairs has, at least temporarily, given way to ideological sight/blindness in such areas as Northern Ireland, the Persian Gulf, and Central America. Indeed, adversarial politics are increasingly operative throughout the world. (Whatever happened to the conditions that motivated the creation, not much more than four decades ago, of the United Nations?) It is not accidental that certain people, especially those historically disadvantaged or those whose privileges seem imperiled by recent developments, distrust those with power over them when those who rule do not share the ideology of the ruled. The powerful and the powerless simply do not, *and cannot*, see reality alike. That is the widespread and, in many ways, frightening realization of the late twentieth century. *People's faith commitments unavoidably influence their understanding of the variety of human experience.* Consequently, there is probably no such reality as universal human experience. Although that acknowledgement may make our immediate task more difficult, it in no way changes my initial contention about the ways in which experience and faith mutually influence each other. Experience, the range of which in any culture is limited by the society's operative faith, endlessly raises questions about the adequacy of any faith formation. There is no way in which the limit-setting and limit-enlarging dialectic will ever cease. This process is independent of the size of the territory covered by the faith community.

EXPERIENCE AS DEFINED BY FAITH

What do I mean by such general categories as experience and faith? Clearly, they both have been used to refer to a vast range of realities, some of which may be incommensurable with others discussed under the same rubric. Thus, the immediate task is to limit as accurately as possible what I intend each term to mean.

In seeking to understand the potential range of human experience, we must recognize that some faith systems encourage, whereas others discourage, greater width and depth of experience. Does it matter for the sake of one's affirmable and pursued experience whether one believes, for example, in the presence of the living God of Scripture or, to use the case of British politics, in the gentle socialism of the current Labour Party or in the unmodified "theology" of Adam Smith of the Conservatives? Might, for example, a lively biblical faith urge one to embrace, as necessary to human experience and certainly to any understanding of it, the value of *both* individual lives and the societies into which all persons are born and from which none is ever fully separated? The politician's persuasive task may be simplified by talking only about individualism *or* community, but is either emphasis adequate to understand human life, including one's own? In terms of the range of experience to which they provide access, the *evaluation* of faith alternatives may prove unavoidable. As those who have been shaped primarily by liberal assumptions, in the same way that we are reassured by every evidence of reasonableness and moderation, we are made uneasy by manifestations of irrationality and excessiveness. But, apart from ideological necessity, does our experience manifest only reasonableness and moderation? If there is more to our experience than that, how do we make sense of it? Or do we refuse that task in favor of seeing only what conforms to our assumptions about reality?

It is tempting for those more educated to assume that because they are familiar with the idea of a range of experience encompassing, for example, both the rational and the irrational, they are in touch with these dissimilar realities in their experience. Having spent most of my adult life as part of a college faculty, I am quite suspicious of that assumption. Although there are those with extensive formal education who recognize the presence and influence of irrationality in their personal and public lives, it does not follow that extensive formal education assures such insight. For reasons inherent in the nature of such education, such as its emphasis on objectivity and on tasks in which reason—often only a limited kind of mathematical rationality—is competent, it is unlikely that the extensively educated will have insight about their own irrationality. Because they have concentrated on reality understood in a certain way and have stressed intellectual competence over social experience, it is no surprise that such people would tend not to recognize irrationality when it erupts in their lives. Their tendency would be to use their considerable intellectual and verbal skills to conceal any such irrationality. It was as a result of thousands of therapeutic hours with others that, in his autobiography, C. G. Jung accused "so-called intellectuals" of being—next to habitual liars—the most difficult patients.[2] In his terms, the underlying problem is the intellectuals' propensity for separating intellect from feelings. Although in my understanding faith is not simply equatable with feeling, I contend that one's underlying faith, such as that of the academic in intellect, determines the extent of one's access to nonintellectual experience. That one may deny the existence, certainly the importance, of that for which one's system has no use does not mean that such experience does not continue to occur and have its impact on lives. Again in Jung's terms, ". . . yet the intellectual still suffers from a neurosis if feeling is underdeveloped."

Often such irrational eruptions occur in the interpersonal realm, in which people are not objects that can be dealt with in purely rational ways, but they may occur in public and professional areas as well. One minor illustration might suffice. A decade ago, in response to rapidly escalating oil prices, a college administrator made an arbitrary but reasonable

decision to begin the academic year earlier in the hope of
saving fuel by scheduling a holiday during part of the winter.
When the administration announced several years later that
the experiment had not resulted in significant energy econ-
omy, the faculty was urged to return to the original schedule.
This schedule allowed students to be at home in December only
for a fortnight rather than for the six weeks of the experimental schedule. The shorter time at home seemed desirable both
for freshmen, one of whose important psychological tasks is to
leave home, and for their parents who had the comparable task
of learning to let go of them. However, the experimental schedule remains in place, in part because, having found ways to
make it serve their purposes, faculty were uninterested in any
adverse effects of a schedule imposed for extrinsic reasons
which had been proven invalid. The unacknowledged irrationality lay in the inability to consider the merits of any proposal
that jeopardized their interests. Although in general I am
comfortable with action based on self-interest, this behavior
seems to be at odds with the assumptions of rationality which
supposedly undergird the academic profession. Argumentation
to the contrary notwithstanding, academicians often have at
least as much difficulty as do others in affirming the full range
of their varied experiences. What does not conform to the
liberal/rational assumption—anger, envy, or lust—is either
denied or rationalized away. Something out of the ordinary is
needed to motivate greater inclusiveness. It is to that extraordinary something that we may now turn.

Having contended that political and educational faith systems both enable us to see certain things clearly and blind us
to others, I want now to propose that Christian faith endlessly
encourages us to embrace ever broader ranges of experience.
That will be an objectionable surprise to faith partisans of
either politics or education, especially if their experience of
religion has been repressive.

Well aware that many forms of organized religion are expe-
rientially restrictive, and perhaps all forms are in varying
degrees or from time to time, I shall not pretend to speak for
all forms of Christianity. There is too much variety for that.

What I do want to do, however, is to argue that *every ecclesiastical effort to conceal or to restrict access to human experience is
contrary to its mission.* Whether motivated by timidity or
prudence, and there are many instances in which these and
other considerations will be appropriately operative, every
effort to limit access to human experience is at odds with a
central affirmation of the Apostles' Creed. There it is advanced
as an integral article of faith that the crucified Christ "descended into hell."[3] What is this if not the insistence that there
is no fragment of human experience with which this Messiah
is not familiar, nothing of which human beings are capable
that may not be redeemed? As the initial article of that Creed
insists, all that exists is of God, however immediately estranged it may appear to be. Not all experience may be desirable for us at certain times of our lives. For example, it may be
imprudent to confront a grieving person with yet more reasons
for grief, but for the Christian there is no human experience
which is utterly alien. Some experiences may be less appealing, or even repugnant, but inasmuch as they have happened
to others, I have no reason for denying their reality. When my
sight is clearest, I am able to recognize within myself at least
the seeds of another's unattractive behavior. In this sense
organized religion exists more to remind us how much like
others we are, however distinctive each is, rather than how
much unlike them we appear to be. Christianity's good news is
that no one is beyond the reach of God's renewing grace, that
the resolve to conceal one's sins is only the next to last word.
The last word is God's determination to forgive acknowledged
sin.

My underlying thesis is that in the interest of being more
lovingly and creatively present to those around me, it is imperative to acknowledge the realities of my life in the flesh. The
less able I am to do this, the less able will I be to provide either
the hospitality or the healing that are among love's central
works. The more in touch I am with the considerable range
(positive and negative) of my experience, the more capable will
I be of these works of love. For the sake of the neighbor and for
the love of God, Christian faith leads us in the direction of

endlessly enlarged experience—the descent into hell. Anything else is an accommodation to some less inclusive cultural ideology.

At least initially, this is not an appeal to enlarge or change one's activities in any dramatic way. That may be a consequence which will eventually have to be addressed. Immediately, however, the assignments are more modest: to recognize how detached we usually are from our daily experience and to begin to identify some of the means that support such detachment.

The symptoms that accompany progressive neglect of one's experience vary greatly among individuals. For example, some people become progressively passive and inert as a result of boredom, yet by the same stimulus others become increasingly restless but without focus for their energy. Given this imaginable range of reactions to self-neglect, it may be more useful to recognize some of the attitudes that keep us at safe distance from any vivid experience. There is a danger that by identifying these attitudes we will, in one sense, contribute to the process of distancing. It may indeed be impossible to enumerate and illustrate the infinitely varied ways in which people keep their experience sufficiently remote so as to enable them to avoid any change. Yet although descriptions of general attitudes that help one to avoid experience may contribute to that avoidance, they may also be the means by which some people become aware of long-established personal habits.

Let me admit also that I am not sanguine about the ease, or likely success, of this assignment. Every society is, I suspect, set up in ways that encourage only certain kinds of experience. However purportedly free a society may be, the reality is that the range of approved or approvable experience is limited. There are only certain attitudes that a given society can tolerate, therefore only those experiences are permitted which are thought to contribute to the formation of those attitudes. Whether or not it is even appropriate to refer to socially prescribed behavior as experience is a question we must at least acknowledge at this point. Certainly the *zeitgeist* is most difficult to recognize—except in retrospect. For something to qualify as (distinctive) experience, does it have to be the result of a certain individual initiative? For example, when running with the wind while sailing one may be unaware of the breeze that moves the boat along. Tacking is a much more compelling illustration of the experience of wind. Does it follow that being somewhat against the grain makes it easier to be aware of what may be happening?

In a stimulating recent essay a fellow Minnesotan seems to think so. Poet and iconoclast, Bill Holm writes thus:

> Sacredness is unveiled through your own experience and lives in you to the degree that you accept experience as your teacher . . . perhaps particularly if it comes into conflict with the abstract received wisdom that power always tries to convince you to live by. *One of power's unconscious functions is to rob you of your own experience* by saying: we know better, whatever you may have seen or heard . . . we are principle, and if experience contradicts us, why then you must be guilty of something. [Whereas I say,] Put your arms around everything that has hampered you, and give it an affectionate squeeze. [emphasis added][4]

There is, of course, a vast range of what goes by the name of potential experience. From this reading it follows that faith lives in all individuals to the extent that they "accept experience as . . . teacher." Are we instructable in any other "classroom"?

One particular sentence in Dag Hammarskjöld's *Markings* deserves inclusion at this juncture: "Never, for the sake of peace and quiet, deny your own experience and convictions."[5] Given his sophisticated mind, his apparent failure to distinguish clearly between experience and convictions may surprise some readers. Although that matter requires clarification, the real surprise here is the importance he attaches to experience. For that we can be grateful. His apparent inability to voice such important convictions publicly while he lived is to be regretted. Only in his posthumously published journal do we discover his emphasis.[6]

Few people, however, readily recognize the incommensurate

nature of his two categories. Depending on their strength, convictions determine experience for most people. Their fundamental assumptions—what I call their faith—define what of reality they may see and enter into. At what point, for example, will the American myth about the denouement of our involvement in Vietnam allow us to acknowledge defeat? In one sense it is heartening to observe the Russians playing the same pathetic tunes in regard to Afghanistan. The nation-state does not easily, if ever, admit failure.

THE DIALECTIC OF FAITH AND EXPERIENCE

One of the questions that arise from my emphasis on the importance of reconnecting with our experience seems in special need of clarification. Some readers may understand me to be making experience a self-justifying end. Certainly, that has been the temptation in all classic mysticism and is the distinguishing feature of all monasticism. That tendency is neither necessary nor is it my intent. No single experience, neither that notably religious nor any quantity of recovered experience, is self-justifying or absolute. It is not to that end that I am exploring the nature of human experience. It is to avoid such absolutizing that the chapter is entitled "Experience *and* Faith." Whether or not there is one normative mode for relating these dimensions of our total lives I do not know. That we are capable of both I take to be evidence of God's gracious presence. That is the source from which both derive: they reveal the good Creator. Their relationship seems to be more dialectical than controlled from either side. Experience determines faith no more than does faith determine experience, though both are the other's primary stimulant and corrective. Neither is an end in itself; each exists for the sake of the other. Creation is not one-sidedly dependent on redemption, nor vice versa; yet they are necessary to each other.

Perhaps it is more accurate to say that although Christian faith does not determine experience, it may be the key to determining how much of our experience we are able to affirm. Irrespective of the extent or the supposed normalcy of our experience, the task is to be able to acknowledge whatever has happened to us and to see its influence in shaping the persons we have become. By this acknowledgement, or need to acknowledge, two things come into clearer focus: our kinship with others and our need for God's forgiveness. As we are so healed (made whole), we are more ready to affirm our connection with others.

Although both experience and faith are imperiled in an era like the present, characterized primarily by a combination of passivity and ideology, including the strident ideologies of some faith communities, I am here stressing the importance of recovering some of one's largely lost experience. Faith in God's forgiveness accompanies the ability to recover that experience but does not automatically issue in the search. That faith may be diverted to many other activities, which fail to deepen it, is why I emphasize in Chapter 4 the work of self-reclamation. As one undertakes this work one discovers both the unauthenticity, or at least the superficiality, of much of one's professed faith and the need for a more encompassing or more incisive faith than was required by one's limited prior self-acquaintance. The more experience one has had, the more urgent are the challenges to one's faith. After all, faith at its best was adequate to *yesterday's* experience. It enabled one, as it were, to assent meaningfully to all that had occurred in one's life up to that time. Assuming the continuity of lives it is reasonable that, in general, faith will continue to be adequate to affirm further experience. It is doubtful, however, that faith ever remains—even from one uneventful day to the next—completely unchanged. And at times such will be one's highly eventful experience that the understanding of one's faith will have to be dramatically modified. Experience and faith are in endlessly dialectical relationship. Each is meaningless without the other. Experience becomes a string of unrelated series of events, adding up to nothing, except as it is integrated by faith into the ensemble we recognize as a *human* life. Without this integrative task faith is comparatively empty. Faith is no more end in itself than is experience. Both need and help to make sense of the other.

Apart from its ability to enable one to affirm ever more of

one's experience, faith has no independent value. The difficult
human task is not to have "faith in God," which can mean
many things, or even faith in one's neighbor, which may or
may not appear to be warranted. *The difficult task is to be able
to have appropriate faith in one's unavoidably ambivalent experience.* The ultimate challenge, the paradigm of which is seen
in Jesus' Gethsemane to Golgotha experiences, is whether or
not one will be able to affirm God's presence in adverse experience. Little of significance is involved in a "good times" faith;
misfortune in its myriad forms is the test of faith. By affirming
that experience I do not mean complete approval of it; rather,
affirmation means minimally to acknowledge that certain
things actually happened. Inability so to affirm experience
requires one to deny and to conceal. Concealment of the truth
from others is bad enough; *to have to deny it to oneself is to
pretend to be other than one is.* As in instances of academic
plagiarism, the evil of the self-concealment we are discussing
is that one's very being is being misrepresented. The plagia-
rizer subtly acknowledges the inadequacy of his or her own
views, the pretender says that it is unacceptable to be oneself.
Although many people feel this way about their lives, their
number in no way validates their pretense. There is an alternative way to be present to oneself and world. In the long run
at least, and I suspect ordinarily sooner than that, nothing is
more perilous to oneself or imperiling to others than pretense.
It is as serious as counterfeit coinage is to economic trust.
What makes life "go" is not the amount of pretense we can
persuade others to believe about us; the basis of enduring
reliability is the presence of but a minimum of denial and
concealment. When what is real or important changes constantly, others are kept off balance. Nobody makes his or her
best contribution amid such uncertainty: the self's resources
cannot be brought to bear constructively on any situation in
which trust cannot be established.

Of equal importance in the emphasis on being in touch with
one's experience is that we *not* absolutize that experience. I
emphasize such reclamation not in order to suggest how, for
example, ecstasy recalled may enable us to step out of history.

Whereas such experience of discontinuity is part of the human potential, it is ordinarily an infrequent happening and its effect is fleeting. This is not to discredit the occasional break with the familiar which *can* happen, as easily at the Lord's Table as anywhere else. The point is, acknowledging the exceptions with gratitude, to recognize two things: (1) how out of touch we ordinarily are with the vast range of our experience and (2) how thoroughly we are *in our experience* the products of the society into which we have been born and reared. Public convictions are covertly powerful determiners of experience. This discovery of the continuity of our lives with those of others who share our origin will not necessarily please us, but the displeasure may be the point of God's opportunity to enlarge or somewhat redirect our capacity for experience. Whether we are pleased or otherwise, the goals of reclaiming our lives are twofold: to assent to the overwhelming continuity of our lives with those of others and to recognize both in that continuity and in the much less frequent discontinuity, the gracious presence of God. It is by assenting to our kinship with others and our limited uniqueness that we learn that the love of God may be present to us both in life's ordinary continuities and in the rarer instances of discontinuity. Conversely, in the boredom of continuity and the anxiety of discontinuity we may be aware only of God's absence.

Although this emphasis on the importance of self-acquaintance has deep biblical warrant, it may be unfamiliar to many people. Most of us who are the products of Christian formation through church education programs have been quite consistently discouraged from taking ourselves seriously. We were taught that God and neighbor were proper objects of attention. Self, apparently, either did not need cultivation or would take care of itself. Both are perilous assumptions and are part of the reason that many so-called Christians are ill equipped for life in the modern world. We need to be clearer about that world, because the shape of contemporary life is significant for the emphasis on selfhood as a responsibility commensurate with and inseparable from love of God and neighbor. The imperative for this work arises both from scripture and from developments distinctive of our times.[7]

THE EXPERIENCE OF PLURALISM

Most important of such evidence is a rapidly emerging pluralism. Such is the nature of contemporary life with its high mobility, exposure to a variety of values and practices, erosion of convictions once believed absolute, and, consequently for some, a reversion to antirational authoritarianism, deepening extremes of wealth and poverty—that the inescapability of *choice* is much more central to many people's experience than ever before. Probably at no time or place has life for long been completely uniform. The vagaries and the genius of the human spirit preclude the likelihood that everybody will experience everything identically. A universal illustration is to be seen in the different perspectives that a man and a woman bring to the delivery of their children. Both may want to be parents, but, if only because of the changes occurring in the woman's body, there is no way that their desires or the birth of their child can mean the same thing to both.

Consider also two other illustrations of reactions to pluralism, responses to the Jewish presence in medieval Europe. At the top of the main street of Riquewihr, a small walled village in the wine-rich Rhine Valley, there is a sign, *Juif Strasse.* As in many comparable settlements in Western Europe, this sign is a reminder that Christendom was never a seamless social fabric. The purpose of the sign long ago may have been to isolate the strangers, but it is also a reminder today that there were other-than-Christians throughout Europe.

The uneasiness of Christians in the presence of those who did not share their outlook—ignoring at the moment the varieties of theology and practice within "Christendom"—is more sharply revealed by a sign posted on the only surviving building of a once huge abbey outside the Oxford Westgate. There, assumedly, both to report certain unacceptable facts and to serve as a caution to others who might be comparably tempted, was the record of a man of Christian origins who did the then unacceptable deed of falling in love with a Jewish woman.

Near this stone in Osney Abbey
Robert of Reading,
Otherwise, Haggar of Oxford,
Suffered for his [Jewish] faith
on Sunday 17 April 1222 A.D.
Corresponding to the Year 4982 A.M.

Although I am permanently less than sanguine about the
resurgence of anti-Semitism, I doubt that we are disposed to
"ghetto-ize" Jews in the way of those who designated the *Juif
Strasse*. Nor, I trust, is there ecclesiastical disposition to burn
at the stake a Christian who may choose to convert to Judaism
for whatever reason. Anti-Semitic jokes and attitudes persist,
however, and the potential for destructiveness against Jewish
property and people lies just beneath the surface; acts of
discrimination erupt too often to warrant anything but vigi-
lance. Such hostility may be fired in Christians by the challenge inherent in the tradition of Abraham, which is mother
to both Islam and Christianity. The continued presence of Jews
is an ancient reminder of the need for choice so widely characteristic of the modern world. Anti-Semitism is a reaction of
those whose self-acquaintance is too meager to enable them to
appreciate the merits and demerits of an alternative faith
system. Pluralism may as easily result in pogroms and tribal
contests as in searching into the adequacy of others' belief
systems and of one's own. Tolerance is one of the most fragile
of the modern virtues; dialogue-as-a-virtue has yet to achieve
any widespread acceptance.

Despite the verbal importance attached to choice, the privilege of the educated, we deceive ourselves if we claim great
importance for the opportunity to decide where nothing significant is at issue: for example, which *good* college to attend? or,
for which profession to prepare? Such nonexistential matters
constitute the pretense of decision. Where a choice searches
the depths of one's being, where self-knowledge is requisite to
the choice, most of us would be grateful for a way out. Sometimes there is no escape ramp; a hard choice is inescapable.
One of the great novels to emerge from World War II was

Nicholas Monsarrat's *The Cruel Sea.*[8] Late in his story of HMS
Compass Rose, an anti-submarine vessel without convincing
evidence of a "kill" after several years of North Atlantic duty,
the captain is faced with an impossible but inescapable choice.
He sees a German submarine sink one of the cargo ships in the
convoy on its way to Gibraltar. With sonar equipment he
determines that the submarine is sitting on the ocean floor
immediately below many survivors of the torpedoed ship. The
conflict between the desire to rescue one's friends and the
opportunity to destroy an enemy capable of endless destruction
has rarely been drawn more sharply or more painfully.

The ubiquity of unavoidable choice mandates a level of self-
awareness never before needed by all. To make something
positive out of pluralism's potential will require a rare willingness to pay the price of self-knowledge. Unacceptable alternatives to such acquaintance are either to refuse to live in this
kind of world or to strike out at those who are different. In a
rare interview on the occasion of his son's birthday, Tom
Stoppard, one of England's great contemporary playwrights, is
quoted thus: "I do believe in God, whatever that means, but I
don't belong to any religion, and I'm not a churchgoer. I have a
strong sense of what I think is right and wrong. But acting on
it doesn't exactly follow. You can act as badly as anyone else.
You just feel guiltier about it."[9] Although few have Stoppard's
talent, many would not be uncomfortable having his religious
self-description applied to themselves. Discomfort arises at the
point where one realizes that the failure to act on the basis of
what one knows to be right has resulted in death or meaningless misfortune for others. When the choice is between self-
awareness and holocaust for a certain minority, is there really
a choice? It will not do for the sake of the future of the present
world for people to refuse to claim their experience and to
recognize its implications for how they may relate to others.
Willful self-ignorance will, predictably, issue in hostility
against those who are different.

In addition to its importance as a precondition for life together amid divisive pluralism, self-acquaintance has at least
as much importance for individuals coming to grips with what

it is they really believe. Underlying the desire for a modicum
of social harmony while honoring others' diverse views is
people's need for self-acquaintance as they sort out what really
does and does not matter to them. At least in the Western
world, although the ubiquity of the media assures that there
are few places of escape anywhere, it is increasingly uncom-
mon for men and women to remain unchanged throughout life
as members of the faith family into which they were born.
Even when they continue comfortably to wear the family's
religious label, the content of that tradition will undergo many
changes over the course of a lifetime. What difference does it
make to one's faith to learn that one has lived through an era
distinguished by such diverse events as the Holocaust of World
War II, the dropping of the atomic bombs on Hiroshima and
Nagasaki, a worldwide population explosion, and determined
campaigns by a handful of people in many countries to protect
the environment from "developers" and to save a variety of
imperiled animal species? The present and foreseeable world
is, in many ways, unlike the world into which I was born. So
fundamental are some of the changes that it is extremely
difficult not to recognize their unsettling effects on my understanding and commitments. Can I, for example, continue to
ignore the powerful influence television must have on young
people in particular? Given the extent of children's exposure
to the media and to popular music, how will they distinguish
between reality and fantasy? How similar will their understandings be to those of people raised before the advent of
radio?

For good and ill the world changes, with the result that not
only *how* but *what* we experience cannot remain unchanged.
In addition to such changes in the external world, however,
there are variations in experience itself over a lifetime. For
example, a person's sense of mortality at age sixteen is unlikely to be the same as at age sixty. The particular assumptions about mortality operative during adolescence, and appropriately unsettling for those years, have vastly less
applicability four or five decades later. Although the passage
of time may not influence all other areas of one's life, it cannot

be without influence on the feelings associated with the awareness that one will not live forever. Both the adolescent's and
the aging person's feelings about this subject may be valid for
their respective ages; the point is that we *not* claim the superiority of one or the other. Rather, as such changes occur,
especially when they come about gradually and perhaps imper-
ceptibly, it is urgent to recognize that there have been changes
and to adjust our theology accordingly. A theology adequate
for adolescence—or whatever a faith system in those years
might be called—will never endure unchanged to aging and
death. Experience of change requires appropriate modifications of one's belief system.

It is for these reasons, both those distinctive to the late
twentieth century and those inherent in the maturation required at all times, that willful self-ignorance is never recom-
mended. Where choice is unavoidable, as is urgently the case
today, the options are frightening. One's choices will accompany or result from improved self-knowledge, which is ob-
tained through a painful process not made easier because of
its urgency. If the hard work of progressive self-acquaintance
is refused, people will face a grinding ideological warfare akin
in costliness to that of the trenches in the Great War. Given
the current resurgence of certain ideologies it is easy to argue
for a tragic view of the human experiment.

THE VULNERABILITY OF FAITH

The problem is that we are averse to being vulnerable, and
there is no way to undertake the process of self-acquaintance
while remaining invulnerable. In the process of reclaiming our
experience, of substituting more accurate recollections for illusions or faulty memories, we must set aside, at least temporarily, the ordinary roles which shield us. Doing so may be
recognized as a desirable process for enabling us to mature,
but it is not for that reason desired by anybody. The more
thorough the process of review/reclamation, the more vulnerable one becomes. At some point one either abandons the project
or reaches *for a depth of faith that incorporates vulnerability in
its understanding of the nature of ultimate reality*. While no

belief system requires the adherent to become vulnerable, central to Christianity is the insistence that, in Christ crucified, God became vulnerable to all of the destruction of meaning of which anti-God forces are capable. Thus, the crucifixion/ resurrection becomes the event which, when entered into, frees one to persist in the painful and supremely rewarding work of self-acquaintance. In this process vulnerability is unavoidable. Paradoxically, vulnerability, once demythologized—that is, its threat somewhat deflated by a faith that incorporates vulnerability as intrinsic to life in the world under God—becomes the means for the reclamation of ever more of one's experience. Something is going on here of which we are ordinarily unaware. It may be this: that the more experience we are able to reclaim, the more capable we become of both further reclamation and of further experience. The Christ who descended into hell is not frightened by any experience we may bring to him.

One of the passages in the Gospels about which I have the most ambivalent feelings is Jesus' explanation of his use of parables. From one side of my being I am put off by his suggestion that this pedagogy best accomplishes his purpose. Some of the hearers would be instructed by the parables; others would either learn nothing of import or only be amused. Those who could already "see" would see more clearly; those whose *present* sight was at best dim would see even less. (see Matthew 13:10–13). Egalitarian assumptions make this unacceptable.

Yet there is an excruciating truth here: what may open one person's eyes will allow another to sleep on. The question I have often asked myself as minister, teacher, person of faith, is this: What might prove instructive? At the very least I have concluded that no one thing works for everybody. That there are "different strokes for different folks" has become true for me as I have lived longer. (A minor consolation about Jesus' use of parables has been the realization that other aspects of his ministry may have touched the imagination of those who were either confused or entertained by his stories.) No single method will assuredly arouse all people. Just what it will take to bring people to their senses simply cannot be known in advance. What we can do if we want to enlarge and deepen people's experience, is to identify just what social forces may be discouraging them. Until we know about the resistances and are able to take account of them, the effectiveness of our efforts will be limited.

The constant resistance is aversion to change. As long as things remain as they are—which, of course, they don't, either in life or on stage—most people will not be moved to change them. Thus is limited experience diminished again and again. *The* question, which Paul asked repeatedly, is: "Who will rescue me from this body of death?" (Romans 7:24). When we really mean the question, hope arises. The trouble is, as with many gestures we make, we often discover that we do not really mean it.

And what is it that makes clear our lack of deep intent? Is it not that we fail to see that the changes required of us will result in an improved situation? We might like the gain if it were cost-free. However, we are put off by the asking price of risk and costly change. The need for something different, for an improvement in a constantly deteriorating condition, has to be imperious enough to cause us, with Paul, to cry out for help. That cry, rather than the suffering inherent in our present condition, is the precondition of any lasting change. Suffering as such may simply progressively dull our sensibilities. There needs to be the willingness, even as we try to understand the experience, so to undergo the suffering that we may be changed by it.

These are hard words, not to be spoken glibly. They are, however, at the heart of the Christian gospel and underlie what I have tried to say about experience *and* faith. I am struck again by the power of the events of Holy Week. At his crucifixion, at which time he obviously continued to try to understand, crying "My God, my God, why have you forsaken me?" (Matthew 27:46), Jesus had to have experienced a crucial transition. Beyond the effort to understand what was happening there was the need to embrace the experience as from God. The cry of dereliction from the cross was an integral human question: *the desire to understand one's experience is almost the last word.* Fortunately for us, he went beyond it to acceptance:

"It is finished." (John 19:30) If we are able to say anything with certainty about the relationship of the historic Jesus to the Christ of faith it has to be at this point. God saw fit to raise Jesus from the dead because, for reasons we will never know for certain, Jesus moved through and beyond the desire to understand, to the embrace of that experience. In that he was changed. In him, so may we hope for ourselves. Whatever may have kept him initially from entering fully into the experience of his own death—Scorcese's suggestion in *The Last Temptation of Christ* may be right—had to be overcome if the final change required of him was to be possible.

In Jesus, then, we have the paradigm of the ultimate tension between experience *and* faith. God would move us into ever deeper experience, which we resist because we are not sure but that the price is excessive. Only as we are ever more willing to embrace further experience (or is it as we are first given faith which enables that embrace?) do we encounter the mystery wherein these basic components of human life dwell. That mystery believers call the gracious God. Therein we can affirm experience and faith.

Ralph Waldo Emerson is credited with an important distinction between different kinds of time, which we may recognize in our own experience, "Some hours have authority over all other hours."[10] Human experience is never uniform. Clock time's uniformity is a construct convenient for aspects of life in a commercialized society. In addition to *chronos*, which was the term they used to describe such time, the Greeks knew from experience a kind of time they called *kairos*, a special time. Such a distinction underlies Emerson's realization that some experiences have the power to order and give meaning to all else.

Such authoritative experience will not be identical for everybody. One person's heightened hour will be flat for another. What causes a particular experience to break out of life's comparative regularity is a topic too large to be other than simply acknowledged here.

In conclusion it must be said that Christians are distinguishable from others in consequence of that Good Friday/Easter experience which is normative for them. Their kinship, which unifies without requiring uniformity, arises from agreement as to which are the authoritative hours. From that faith-accessed experience, they are emboldened to open themselves to ever more varied experience. Terrified by the unfamiliar, they are driven to ground their lives ever more deeply. Thus does the dialectic of experience and faith spiral up and down ever more dizzyingly and inclusively. All this, they believe, to the glory of God.

Chapter 3

Life's "Morning": The Forward Thrust

As members of an activist society—one which routinely prefers action over reflection—many are surprised and somewhat dismayed by the sorts of questions which they find themselves asking at mid-life. The Buddhist might say in a crisis, "Don't do something—stand there!" Just standing there makes us uncomfortable. Rather, we feel as though we should always be doing something, on the understanding that few if any situations cannot be improved, or at least kept from actual deterioration, by forthright action. Even a little activity is often preferred to a lot of reflection. To be busy is deemed praiseworthy.

We readily grasp the last part of Soren Kierkegaard's insightful epigram: "Life can only be understood backwards; but it must be lived forwards." We readily assent to this dynamic insistence to look and live toward the future. Obedience to this exhortation has resulted in incomparable social benefits. The commitment to public education, with college opportunities for all who are even slightly motivated, is but one illustration of a society looking ahead. The mid-nineteenth-century commitment to land-grant institutions of learning was embodied in legislative policy and decision making at the highest level. Those who decided to put public land to such use recognized the social benefits inherent in the opportunity for extended education.

Having personally benefited from this opportunity, I have much admiration for those who fashioned that legislation.

However, I sense also that the activist assumptions underlying it create problems for some of us today. So single-minded is our intent to live toward the future that we are often at a loss to take seriously the other half of Kierkegaard's observation. Confronted with the insistence that life can *only* be understood backwards, we often simply look for something to do as though forward living were our life-long assignment. We often behave as though the morning were the only meaningful part of a human life, as though its agenda had to be pursued in life's afternoon and evening as well. It is as though we believe that the only assignments appropriate to adult men and women are those that call for aggressive action as though an uninterrupted tilt to the future assured eventual understanding of our life.

Without demeaning such behavior, I have discovered that there is more to life than being busy. Activity is but one of several basic components, rather than the normative one, for people at all of life's stages. C. G. Jung has noted that various things matter at different stages of life. The activities in which we invest ourselves early in life do not remain as important when our lives pass beyond "high noon." Jung insists that what was true in the morning becomes a lie in the afternoon.[1] That hyperbole can be a useful exaggeration if it encourages us to open our eyes to what is happening within us. The problem is that the ubiquity and depth of our commitment to the importance of external matters, to activism and to problem solving, may make it impossible to acknowledge inner questions that arise in mid-life. The more ideological the commitments, the more difficult is the acknowledgement that anything may go awry which activity will not rectify. If we cannot/will not hear the questions, we will continue the morning's work, trying to find the satisfactions that once came so readily from it. The pleasure may become ever more difficult to arouse and the rewards limited, but we will persist at the morning's tasks if the prospect of a different assignment remains offputting. Diminished rewards suggest need for a change of focus without requiring it. Experiences of the middle years are not universal and there is no obligation to respond positively to these promptings. Most people probably try to deny that anything has changed—certainly there is no set timetable for all—and many refuse to break the familiar stride. At the least, such successful denial is a misfortune; at the worst, it may be willful deafness to God's call into life's late afternoon.

Without insisting that everybody has to grow old with us, which is as silly as trying to deny that we have aged, we need to be able to hear the questions of life's afternoon as they begin to take shape within us. They are not alien inquiries; they are the good fruit of our experience. Jung's exaggeration about truths becoming lies may be modified to read "Interests and obligations vary in importance from one time to another." For example, the zeal with which we once needed to distinguish ourselves from others, preferably by showing our superiority, subsides somewhat in time. Although it can remain an ingredient in the continuing life of all people and a comparatively important aspiration in the afternoon, even into the evening of some people's lives, this need usually ceases to be central in the configuration of agenda in one's later years. The need to be outstanding is an appropriate preoccupation in a stage of life but gradually it shares importance with some other goals such as cooperation and mutuality. It matters less how unlike others I am when I am discovering the truth and the joy of my likeness to them. Both distinctiveness from and similarity to others remain true to the end, but the emphasis changes from life's morning to the afternoon. Jung's hyperbole is useful if it makes it difficult for us to deny that a transition is occurring. What was true becomes a lie only if we insist that whatever was central in the morning's configuration is the only thing a person of any age may wholeheartedly pursue. Our external appearance is another example. It may never become a matter of complete indifference, but surely it should not continue to wield the imperiousness it exercised during adolescence. One's inner attractiveness might be of increasing interest for one well into adulthood.

The problems with the morning's agenda, which paradoxically may make it difficult for us to move beyond its emphases, are twofold. In many ways, they are quite subtle, and second, perhaps as an accompaniment to the subtlety, they are often experienced as reality itself rather than as cultural constructs appropriate in this society.

However, before turning to some of these morning ingredients, which is but prelude to discussion of the afternoon as a time for claiming our lives, it is important to recognize that the understanding which is our eventual goal will always remain incomplete. Kierkegaard was well aware that life's forward thrust persists to death. Its pace may slow down, but it never stops. Thus, the possibility of complete retrospective understanding is precluded by the dynamic of life's moving endlessly ahead. This predictable incompleteness may further contribute to the societal inclination to stick with morning's agenda. It is not difficult to see why people might prefer to remain with what is knowable and to a certain degree accomplishable, rather than to move toward tasks that will unavoidably remain imprecise and, at best, only partly attainable. Only the experience of diminishing satisfaction from the known will lure some people on to whatever may be their afternoon agenda. It must be emphasized that there are satisfactions in pursuing matters which can never be fully grasped. That reassurance is at some odds with the societal assumption that it is always better to attempt something accomplishable.

Our current enthusiasm for computers illustrates perfectly how problems become defined in ways consistent with the resources available for their solution. Given its construction— the switch is either on or off—the computer is extremely helpful when one is dealing with material which is either true or false. The problem for which the computer is not equipped, which tends to be shunted aside as a nonproblem, is that most important human experiences embody something of both. Ambiguities are inherent in human experience.

We tend to assume that tasks can always be defined in ways that assure some achievement and consequent pleasure. Regrettably, this assumption is both false (we cannot always fashion accomplishable tasks) and at odds with the holistic tasks that are inseparable from life's afternoon and evening. Bits and pieces of information no longer satisfy when the question has to do with whether or not one's experience adds up to a meaningful story.

Without denying that a forward impetus continues to death, though somewhat diminished in one's later decades, I am determined to make as persuasive a case as possible for the work of reflection for which some become increasingly capable in aging. Looking to the future and reflection are not either/or tasks, one of which ceases when the other appears. Both are probably operative throughout life, but each has an appropriate season for being the dominant interest. For example, adolescents are not blind to their mortality, but it would be inappropriate for that to be as important a consideration at sixteen as it may be at age sixty. Similarly, while the aged ordinarily do not lose sexual capability, it would be inappropriate for sex to be as overridingly important at sixty as it often is for the teenager. Consider one of the slogans from the French university struggles of the 1960s, "The young make love; the old make obscene gestures." There is an element of truth, to be sure. Sexual intercourse is not the same act in youth that it is in old age. Such ageist prejudice, however, is noxious. However older people may relate intimately, their ways of communicating will be anything but obscene. They may, for example, take each other vastly more seriously as persons than is within the capability of any sexually self-preoccupied young person. In this all too common illustration of the inadequacy of prejudiced opinion against older people, youth confused a difference with a qualitative evaluation.

THE FORCE OF EXPECTATIONS

One characteristic of life's morning agenda seems overridingly important. It is the fundamental psychological reality of those years: we live out other people's scenarios. Rather than taking our cues from a gradually emerging future, we accept the cues of others' expectations—usually our parents', often our mothers'—for our lives. Rather than fashioning our own dreams, or sensing our own visions, we try to fulfill others' unfulfilled lives. (Ernest Hemingway's response to his Victorian mother's detailed expectations after his return from the

Great War illustrates a son who, for the sake of his soul, had to distance himself from her. More venal are parents who are more covert about their expectations.) Whether a person's response to parental expectations is positive or negative in no way diminishes their influence. The rebellious child's life reflects the parental impact as compellingly as the life of the compliant child. These realities are at least as ancient as Jesus' parable of the prodigal son.

I doubt that it is possible to overemphasize the hopelessness of attempting to fulfill others' unfulfilled lives. For all our sophistication we remain children hoping to be approved by those important persons who may have withheld that approval earlier. Many parents knowingly keep children enthralled to them and their whims, spooning out limited appreciation no matter the size of the achievement. More common are the obligations that children intuit from the family situation. That these intuitions may be right or wrong matters less than that children feel obligated to do something to warrant the affection of mother and/or father. Whether or not parents are ever utterly innocent of burdening the young, I increasingly doubt.

Probably all people have been influenced positively or negatively by family attitudes and expectations. Some suffer lifelong deprivation from parents who, whatever the pretense, lacked enthusiasm for them. There are those children whose lack of eye-hand coordination was an embarrassment to an athletically skilled father or mother. That situation is more common but no less lethal than the experience of many a less-than-talented child of intellectually gifted parents. There seems to be no limit to the number of reasons why parents withhold the affections which alone enable children to get on with the business of their own lives. Parents-as-but-temporary-stewards is a difficult role for many mothers and fathers to learn. In a recent conversation a fifty-year-old demonstrably competent lawyer related: "I went to law school and took up practice here, partly to please my father. It didn't work. Eventually I realized that even a son might have had trouble getting his approval. Even so, at my age, I'm still striving to extract the occasional smile or kind word, preferably both, from him. I know what an emotional tyrant he is but I can't help myself."

These are poignant feelings. Regrettably, most people will have little trouble identifying with them. They may long ago have physically left the parental home without ever having moved out emotionally. They may have married in name without ever transferring their emotional needs from the family of origin to the family of choice. The most serious violation of the biblical basis for marriage, for which a person is more to be pitied than condemned, has been the inability to leave mother and father in order to cleave to his or her spouse. This pitiable condition moves in the direction of sin because of the confusion of one's roles as spouse, parent and child. Ostensibly committed to all of those relationships, promising to give and receive nurturance both to and from one's spouse and children, one is present to those relationships in name only. One remains dependently strapped to the parental emotional exchequer from which it is impossible to draw enough, to say nothing of ever overdrawing. The future toward which one ostensibly lives and toward which one should help one's family to move is in bondage to enduring parental expectations. Even the death of one's parents may not provide the much needed liberation.

For some men and women, however, the first tremors of the need for change signal the onset of what has been called the mid-life crisis. This crisis is marked by the urgent emergence of a different set of questions which prompt some people to see the damaging effects of the emotional patterns they inherited and to begin to take the first, tiny, hesitant steps that will free them from their dependency. Perhaps struck by the realization of how comparatively little time they have left, they become aware of the demonic character of parents who were never able to free their children for life-affirming lives in the world.

I am reminded of the different climate in the homes of two relatives we visited in my childhood. Lacking labels then, I knew only that I liked one and disliked the other. In the latter case, there were always conditions to be met before any limited approval was meted out. I remember wondering about the odd behavior of the children of this family, my cousins. Only later did I learn about the self-destructiveness to which they were driven in their so-called adulthood. Their father conveyed the sense that any next generation would be hard pressed ever to approximate his achievements. Did he really feel that way or was he himself so emotionally deprived that, having done all he could to win approval, without success, he had no choice but to withhold the life which had been withheld from him? It takes little imagination to recognize the truth of the observation that the sins of the fathers are long visited on their children. (As a parent myself decades later, discovering that I could not give to our children what I lacked, my attitude toward my life-withholding uncle ameliorated a bit.)

Is there any question that, short of traumatic and costly change, we perpetuate with our offspring some variation on the deprivations to which as children we were subject? Most people likely vow not to repeat the emotional patterns of their home of origin. We are able to keep any portion of this vow only because we are usually only one of two parents. The curse is that this combination often results in compounding the forms of bondage rather than offering liberation for their children. For reasons that have something to do with why partners select each other, it is rarely the case that the attitudes received in one family setting are counterbalanced by those the other spouse has received. Rather, the burdens descending from one family of origin are *added* to those from the other. Anything but a promising prospect for the next generation! The amazing thing, for which tenacity I thank God, is that boys and girls survive overdoses of parental expectations. The trouble is that it is extremely difficult to become a life-giving adult if one has been the child of life-withholding parents.

In recent years we have heard more than ever before about sexual molestation within families. This is an extreme form of parental exploitation, but different only in degree from the deprivations we have been discussing. Parents who so victimize their children, as they were usually themselves victimized, are often uninterested in opportunities for therapy that might enable them to disentangle some of the twisted errors of their emotional lives. According to one British observer such patterns are reproduced from one generation to another as though such relations were normative.[2]

In accounting for the unwillingness to undertake potentially helpful therapy, one would have to add to such acceptance of incest as normal the difficulty of bringing about change in an adult, even when there is some desire for it. Therefore, it is often necessary to remove children from family settings where they will unavoidably be exposed to exploitation from which they will not easily recover. We do not recover readily from any exploitation to which we were subject as children. Since sexual exploitation involves aspects of our being that we never outgrow, aspects that constantly color all of our relationships thereafter, we may better understand the universal prohibitions against incest. Its victims are rendered incapable of those normal sexual relationships on which the species depends—it is that serious.

FROM MORNING TO AFTERNOON

Having acknowledged what may be the fundamental psychological burden under which many people struggle as they try to live toward the future, we are in a position to identify some of the qualities of human activity in life's morning. By becoming familiar with these we will be better able to appreciate both the importance and the difficulty of the work of our later years which Kierkegaard described as understanding life backwards. It is our task to recognize both the gradual change between agenda of life's morning and afternoon and some of the reasons that many people decline to undertake the distinctive work of the later years. Reflection may always remain a minority activity. Dealing with the realities that underlie the work of self-reclamation may well become the primary spiritual task of Christians at some point beyond life's noon. The point we must not lose sight of is simple and elusive: *life in the spirit is largely a matter of one's attitude toward one's life in the flesh.* The mundane facts of our lives are never ends in themselves. The result of trying to assign them that importance will be despair, rather than the integrity of the mature Christian person.

The mundane facts of our lives, such as our preference for activism over reflection or the heavy hand of the parental past under which many labor, which we often either overemphasize or try to conceal, matter because it is through them that God seeks to fashion us into men and women in the image of God. Any spirituality which we are able to take seriously must address the misuses to which we put our lives. True spirituality cannot be an attempted escape from life's mundane realities, which never really disappear. Rather, lives-in-the-Spirit both affirm our goodness and seek its transformation in the direction of greater wholeness. The Holy Spirit deals with these mundane facts, shepherding them as they surely lead us into mature life. Like sheep that thoughtlessly wander off, thereby both imperiling themselves and diminishing the flock, so the various aspects of our lives often seem to prefer to be separated from each other, rather than be nourishingly related.[3]

This tendency is blatant in the attempt of many academicians to make of intellect an end unto itself. At the other extreme, in some therapeutic contexts, affects are often absolutized. Both tendencies may be understandable enough in context. Training the mind is the primary task of higher education, and helping people to be less victimized by their confused feelings is therapy's essential objective. But the point of all sound learning and therapy, which are certainly different realms, is to bring into existence men and women who appreciate the importance of both mind and heart and are comfortably aware of how these capabilities influence each other. The feeling intellect and the thoughtful heart are of God's image, as neither is apart from the other no matter what the level of development. To reconnect those coordinates which, in particular societies or periods of history, tend to become separated is the Holy Spirit's work with life's mundane ingredients—passion and compassion, chaos and order, Apollo and Dionysus.

Detached from its complementary, each capability may be brought to levels of seeming perfection, the achievement of which is the endless temptation for an activist society. That, so isolated, one element will attempt to dominate the other is less readily recognized. These inclinations illustrate that dangerous human penchant to make an idolatrous end of something which is but a means. This penchant becomes sin when, as always happens, the isolated aptitude seeks power over all else. Over the course of history, most things of quality—physical strength and/or appearance, intellect, erotic properties—have at one time or another been absolutized to their distortion and the peril of all else. It was not ancient Semitic whimsy which heard Yahweh pronounce as a first commandment, "You shall have no other gods before me" (Exodus 20:3). Where God has first honor—where, as Jesus insisted, God is loved with heart, soul, mind and strength—all of these things and their properties may be enjoyed and used for their relative value. Where one of these insists on being of more than relative worth—in our time "the bottom line" seems to be making such claims—we should pray for the shepherding Spirit. However legitimate balanced budgets may be, they are not the keys to the kingdom!

Before turning to some of the important characteristics of life's morning it is necessary to emphasize that, at best, morning's interests are only modified, not replaced, by the transition to life's afternoon. If, as we have emphasized, one of these characteristics of life in its forward-looking decades is precisely its interest in the future, it is not true that one loses all such interest in life's afternoon. The changed emphasis is both gradual and partial. Even in the last day of life a dying person may not lack all interest in the future. It may amount to little more than an expected glass of water or the hoped-for departure of a visitor, but while the clock ticks we cannot expunge future considerations from a human life. For some the concern about the future will even be posthumous: will the deceased's requests be honored? It is never a matter of abandoning the future.

When one lives by the morning's agenda, there is little occasion for reflection. One's time is filled and energy consumed by the tasks of fashioning a career, learning to be part of a family in a new way, discovering the meaning of citizenship and other modes of adult participation. These necessary or voluntary activities are self-justifying. One needs only to

immerse oneself ever more thoroughly in them to discover
their rewards, in varying times and circumstances. Unima-
gined challenges and rewards abound in all areas of adult life.
There are challenges such as acquiring the necessary skills
inherent in one's work or discovering how well-equipped one is
for the demands of interpersonal life in the family. Such
challenges are both intellectual and emotional. The rewards of
doing well in a career or in the work of forming a family are
no less varied and genuine. It is likely that one will never
forget certain achievements of one's young adult years—for
example, a display of calm efficiency in dealing with a professional emergency, a discovery that an important relationship
can move through conflict via patience and forgiveness to new
levels of mutual respect and affection. Such achievements are
not the last word about a life, nor do they constitute its
fulfillment, but they are among the good fruits of those decades
in which one lives primarily with an eye toward the future.
Such modest but real achievements, which most people can
remember without needing to inflate them, are part of one's
protection against self-destructiveness once mid-life's de-
illusionment begins.

In recalling such experiences, people may realize their lives
to be more vacuous than they had thought, yet not utterly
bankrupt. Mid-life's tricky assignment is for us to be able to
realize that change is occurring and overdue without succumb-
ing to despair. Suicide is not an appropriate response to the
discovery that fraudulence has been at least as characteristic
of one's life as integrity. There may have been occasional needs
for reflection during the adult decades but, unless either one's
career or one's marriage were in deep crisis, the focus was
primarily situational and solution seeking. The major commitments of one's life were relatively well established. As such
they took as much time and energy as were available. One
believed that it was proper to give oneself generously to them
and to be appropriately rewarded.

Without appealing to any of the more extreme instances of
people who come to feel that they have failed at the tasks of
adulthood, we may observe that in the course of time there is

at least a sagging of interest in the works in which we invested ourselves for several decades. We do not need to equate mid-life crisis with the instances of burnout featured in popular magazines. Yet, however initially right and satisfying they may have been, situations simply are different after twenty or thirty years. It is not surprising that people change jobs in mid-life, or that some marriages dissolve during those years. The experience of boredom with the all-too-familiar is probably universal. Perspectives change with time's passage.

But despite the millions who change jobs and spouses in the hope of recovering something that was lost along the way, the solution ordinarily does not lie in different employment or a new family. Inasmuch as one remains the same person, such changes are, at best, temporary palliatives. Whatever it was that was lost is irrecoverable: it had something to do with once being *in*experienced. At some point, or better, over a period of time, one ceased to be naive. Although nobody has had or can have all human experience, we all reach a point where we have had enough of it to be able to imagine somewhat accurately the character of the rest. The illusions that were a necessary part of the motivation for undertaking the morning's agenda— the expectations of becoming somebody really important without, of course, losing the fine qualities of the days when we were nobodies or when ours was an idyllic marriage, free, certainly, from all conflict, sadness, and loss—gradually have to be abandoned. They no longer seem as true as we once believed them to be; they no longer motivate and reward. When this happens we reach a period of genuine crisis, both for ourselves and for all those who have been familiar with our old patterns that are changing. Trauma is deep and widespread.

At such a time we have moved irreversibly into life's afternoon. There is no way back to naiveté; innocence is, at best, something we may remember. It dawns on us that we may never have been innocent. What then? Has everything been a sham? done for the wrong reasons? of no value? Those are understandable initial reactions of a person encountering for the first time the questions of mid-life. As such, they explain why these years are so traumatic for many. Mid-life is a time of crisis in the ancient Chinese sense: a time of both judgment/ assessment and opportunity. If experienced as judgment only, crisis leads to self-deception and despair. It is only as opportunity is recognized within the assessment that hope emerges. Self-criticism alone destroys. It is only when courage accompanies the critique that a new direction is possible. For courage may enable us to see that no matter how centrally useful it was for decades and how much it continues as a secondary theme for the balance of life, the stuff of life's morning is past. The futurist dynamic which long empowered us has, for those in life's afternoon, lost some of its appeal. We still have potential, but for different tasks in response to unfamiliar, often uncongenial, questions. Now is a time in which one learns either to live against the grain or, progressively, to become a victim of self-disgust and despair. This is not to suggest that the person who undertakes the questions of life's afternoon is free of such disgust and despair. How could such inoculation be possible for those who discover that they may never have been innocent? One of the startling, and at least initially disturbing, features of life's afternoon is that there is no longer an illusion of clear alternatives. Rather, we realize that it is not possible to have integrity without despair. These complementaries never were separable despite the energy we wasted pretending otherwise. The holistic life of the afternoon and evening embraces integrity and despair, for we have need of both. *To be moving in the direction of an unaccustomed wholeness means only that one's capacity for integrity exceeds one's reasons for self-disgust.* To acknowledge this as an accurate description of one's life, rather than pretending to nothing but goodness, or at least good intentions, is the limited perfection of which one is capable. It is this realization that moves some people in the direction of the God who forgives.

THE TASKS OF THE MORNING

Our task now is to characterize some of the salient features of life's morning. By listing and describing some of the qualities of life-before-noon, we will appreciate some of the differences between the two major periods of the adult life. We may also begin to understand our resistance to making the transition from younger adulthood to mid-life and aging. We resist both because, as suggested above, we have acquired some skills for the morning's work and we tend to prefer the familiar to the different and relatively unknown. One such difference is that the morning's tasks are relatively more completable than those of life's afternoon and evening. For example, although one never ceases to be a parent of one's children there comes a time in most families when offspring are on their own. In a sense, the work of bearing and parenting comes to an end. By contrast, the older person's potentially generative relationship to future generations of men and women never ceases. Or, from another aspect of life, preparation for and carrying out a career eventually come to an end, but there is no prospect of concluding one's retirement short of death. We may expect to see more clearly the differences between these two times of our lives while we are familiarizing ourselves with some significant qualities of the morning.

Not necessarily in order of importance, here are a half dozen unavoidable attributes of those decades in which men and women are propelled toward the future: through primary concentration on external accomplishments one's inner life is neglected; the assumption of control over one's affairs obscures those aspects of life over which control is impossible; there is a preference for the manageable part over the whole of anything; by appealing much more regularly to will power than to grace we experience a fatigue hard to explain; through recourse to ideology we attempt to conceal myriad uncertainties; rather than acknowledge our imperfections we feign an imperviousness to criticism. There may well be other important qualities of life-in-the-making, but these should suggest the differences between morning and afternoon.

In understanding these polarities of human growth no judgment need be made about their respective values. Both are equally necessary to human maturation. Although in many areas of human achievement that which comes later is thought to be superior to that which it follows, such evaluation is inappropriate here. What I emphasize is that at some indeterminable point in a person's life, for which mid-life is a conveniently vague label, there begins the somewhat new work of gathering together some of the numerous threads of his or her earlier life. Through this reclamation a fabric can be fashioned which others will recognize as reasonably like the person's life. By emphasizing this gathering together I intend no judgment on the self-scattering that took place in earlier decades. Both activities are spiritually appropriate at their respective times of life. Those who are discovering life's afternoon are more interested in discovering the shape their story has taken over the decades than in how much they can yet shape it.

The most noticeable of the qualities of life's morning is the *emphasis on external accomplishments*. Although a person's physical being has never been unimportant—consider all the training individuals experience even before entering school—his or her body becomes yet more important with the onset of puberty. With those glandular and chemical changes children become, overnight as it were, young women and men. I shall not attempt to review the range of tormenting and tormented preoccupation with externals that characterize those adolescent years. Recall, however, the importance for both sexes of the appearance of one's skin; and for girls, the importance of breast development—those with too little unable to imagine the anguish of those with too much and vice versa; for boys, the overriding importance of physique, sports ability, eye-hand coordination. None of this is ever unimportant; none remains as important as we once thought.

The body's importance then became something of a predictor of preoccupations with externals which would continue to characterize people's lives for decades. "Acquiring" is the operative word to describe that next period of life, for what was being accumulated ranged from property to the widest variety of experience. The years between adolescence and mid-life may be unavoidably and without criticism so characterized. The sheer quantity of formal education required of doctors, for example, illustrates the twin assumptions that more is necessary and more equals better. The current mania for travel illustrates the yearning that underlies the desire for yet wider experience. We are surfeited with accounts of the numbers of marriages, to say nothing of liaisons, of some of those who are reportedly today's "beautiful people." Is it surprising that a society with such an aesthetic arouses its critics? Interest in quantity, whatever it may be measuring, tends to conclude that at some point it becomes quality. This assumption is among those that come up for critical review at mid-life.

One of the best of such reviews that I know of is to be found in E. B. White's short story, "The Second Tree from the Corner."[4] Although several other themes are at work in this tale of a man troubled enough to visit a psychiatrist, the story hinges on a role reversal. After many sessions in which the patient finds himself retreating in his chair as the doctor moves towards him, the doctor begins to withdraw as the patient peppers him with questions. The climax comes when Mr. Trexler repeats the question with which the doctor has often driven him to submission, "What, then, do *you* want?" In time the doctor acknowledges that an additional wing for his house in Westport would round out his life nicely. With this disclosure Trexler begins to recover: through the unintended therapy, he knows that he is not as bad off as he had thought. He has his troubles; no doubt about it. But he realizes that troubles like his may be unavoidable and that such a doctor as this could never be expected to help him—or anybody. To assume that more is better is one of those unavoidable illusions of life's morning from which only growing older may rescue us.

The second characteristic of life's morning can be briefly stated and may require little elaboration: in adulthood's early decades *we seek a measure of control and undertake to shape the future.* In a sense, of course, only a small minority of the world's privileged can assume some ability to shape the future. Most people, even in the flush of their youth, may not be bitter about their prospects but are bitterly resigned to a world they neither made nor can significantly influence. Many feel a great deal of hostility because of such a sense of impotence.

Others find ways of modifying their initial assumptions about their ability to "make" the future. What eventually undermines one's sense of control is a combination of unfore-

seeable public events, often in remote places, and one's inheritance. By the latter I refer less to the family's fiscal resources
than to its genetic heritage. Not long ago I heard a woman in
her mid-fifties, apparently in good health, say that both of her
parents had died by the time they were her age. She was quite
concerned by this realization, as I suspect a person would not
have been a quarter century earlier when people did not expect
to live as long. To what conditions and addictions we will
become subject in a comparatively few years is relatively impossible to predict. Contrary to the assumption of continued
good health, we have extremely limited control over our physical or emotional well-being. There are some things that prudence advises and others it warns against, but some factors
are genetically determined and not within our control (for
example, see Matthew 6:27).

When they do not radically shatter us, catastrophic events
may gradually undermine our earlier sense of being in control.
Several events of my childhood and youth, only one of which
had a dramatic influence on me at the time, had devastating
effects upon people who may have thought they were in control:
the stock market crash of 1929, the outbreaks of poliomyelitis
in the thirties, the attack on Pearl Harbor and the years of
war. These and other public events produced casualties. In our
own time probably nothing is more terrifying than the AIDS
epidemic. Virtually unknown less than a decade ago, its impact
on people's sense of control has already been devastating. On a
Sunday in June 1987, I had two compelling reminders of the
prevalence of the virus. In the morning I opened *The Sunday
Times* of London to discover the entire magazine section devoted to the AIDS phenomenon. That evening I attended Even-
song at one of the Oxford colleges and read the following on
the back of the weekly calendar:

AIDS and the Chalice

Questions are being asked about the possibility of developing AIDS through drinking from the cup at Holy Communion. We have been advised that the AIDS virus is
found in saliva only in minute quantities and that the

only way the it could cause infection in another person
drinking from the same cup would be if that person had a
cut lip or a sore mouth. Even then, we are told, it is
extremely unlikely that the virus would be present in a
sufficient quantity to cause infection; and there is no
evidence that this has in fact ever happened.

There is a way of receiving both the bread and the wine at
Communion that avoids contact with the cup; it is called
Intinction: accept the bread and hold it in your hand until
the cup comes; then dip the bread in the wine and receive
both together.

We would like it to be known that we at the Cathedral
regard intinction and the more traditional way of receiving the cup as equally acceptable.

Anyone wanting to talk about this further, or needing
advice or information, should see any of the Cathedral
clergy; we shall be glad to help in any way we can.

Christ Church Cathedral, Oxford

The third feature of life's morning is the highly *selective
emphasis on parts of things rather than on the wholes*. This
attention to component parts, which is the key to successful
industrialization, seems to transfer nicely to human life. Thus,
at work we may concentrate on intellectual skills, even those
of an increasingly specialized kind. Neither interpersonal qualities, nor an aesthetic sense, nor even ethical sensibilities have
any place in a work setting where the product is known, the
means of production are in place, and the "bottom line" determines all. Specialization emphasizes efficiency over completeness. We look to areas other than the workplace for opportunities to exercise those aspects of ourselves that are deemed
valueless on the job. Lives are thus rigorously segmented.

To sustain the assumption that there is always something
that can be done, one must be able to disassemble complex
entities into discrete elements about which it is possible to act.
So long as these entities are physical, preferably mechanical,

the effort remains reasonable. When the organic, especially the human, is involved, dismantlement becomes unacceptable.

In the interpersonal realm the preference for parts is usually dysfunctional. In any significant friendship the other person is unwilling to settle for only that part of us that we consider to be our best side. For any relationship to become and remain important to both parties it must move, however cautiously, in the direction of ever-greater inclusiveness. Humans are wonderfully, sometimes frustratingly, complex beings of body, mind and spirit. Because we are able by memory and imagination to reach from the present moment infinitely into both the past and the future, there is no way that offering only a part of the self will satisfy the needs and demands of a friendship.

In friendship so understood we have the best illustration of what is meant by speaking of persons made in God's image. To be made in the image of God means many things, but none more important than these: the ability to value another person as ourselves, to seek mutual rather than controlling or passive relationships with others, to view others as ends rather than as means to any supposed objective. Underlying these qualities of interpersonal friendship are coordinate assumptions about God. Key to the understanding of the biblical religions is the assumption that, however graceless and obnoxious their behavior, God never relates to persons other than as ends in themselves. All of the glory of the Western humanistic tradition is grounded in that belief, that persons are ends rather than means to other ends. Although often violated, this conviction prompts protests at any effort in a friendship to substitute a part of oneself for the whole.

A book review summarizes the issue: "Commenting in the early 1900's on the evolution of baseball [from the cruder English game of rounders], Argus Evans wrote, 'Americans have a genius for taking a thing, examining its every part and developing each part to its utmost.' "[5] Widely applied in other areas of human experience, this genius for separating parts from the whole is less entertaining than our national game.

The fourth attribute of the style of life's morning may be but a variant on the substitution of a part for the whole. We may call it the *"best self" mentality*. The desire in self-presentation to conceal one's unattractive features is urgent and widespread in a society in which people's opinion of themselves is largely determined by what they perceive to be others' opinion of them.

In an era of other-directedness it is essential to look one's best. This imperative prompts people early in life not to reveal themselves. Because of this instruction, often repeated over the years, boys and girls become men and women skilled in the art of partial self-presentation. We do this in most life situations, such as when we want to impress a peer or prospective employer, when we desire something and sense what might please the person capable of awarding that which we desire, in our relations with those who know us limitedly, where "best self" works best, and even within our families where it is temporarily efficacious in deceiving our children. All spouses and most adult kin are incapable of being so deceived, but we often pretend otherwise in the interest of avoiding immediate collisions.

Rarely acknowledged is the fact that this form of self-justification is made necessary by the erosion of confidence that God alone justifies. Perhaps only in rare moments of religious candor do we acknowledge both the inaccuracy and the inappropriateness of our selective self-presentations. About such inaccuracy I assume nothing more needs to be said. By "inappropriate" I mean that fulfillment of the suppressed desire to be known more fully, as we really are, is rendered impossible by the habit of offering some part of ourselves as though it were the whole person. Under the right conditions, which include the discovery that acknowledging before God our less-approved qualities is not futile, we may see how the development of every relationship is limited by the extent of our self-presentation. Such confinement may be recognized as painfully inappropriate long before, if ever, it may be possible to enlarge the self-presentation. This is not an argument for merely "best self" presentation, which is as faulted as its opposite and for the same reason. Both inflation and deflation conceal the complex person each of us is. This complexity and the ambiguousness that underlies it need to be acknowledged so that relationships can mature. Thus may energies presently needed for the work of concealment be released for greater benefit to all. It is only in our wholeness that we may come before God, in whose image we are said to have been made. Selective self-presentation is unacceptable in this context; its attempted self-justification is too blatant and odorous. Only in the confidence or, at least, with the hope that God is merciful may we come into that Presence in our genuine vulnerability. In that moment we may discover that there is no human condition other than this and that our vulnerability is not fatal. Indeed, once demythologized, that vulnerability is the means to deepen relations with others, with God, and with ourselves. Ultimately, we must rely upon grace for acceptance of our whole self, rather than will power to assert our "best self."

Unfortunately, it is possible for some people well into life's afternoon to continue to prefer pretense to self-disclosure. Many, however, who have borne for decades the burden of pretending to be other than they are want to get out from under that load. Perhaps they have also discovered that "best self" presentation does not assure the approval of those they wished to impress. Whatever their instructive experiences, many older people are in the process of learning to substitute the whole for the part. Less anxious about others' approval, the caprices of which are now better understood, they are increasingly inclined to be themselves, letting others decide what to do about aspects of the person they may not like.

There is no way that we may either persist with satisfaction in partial self-presentation or be uniformly liked as self-presentation is enlarged. There are limitations, however our life is fashioned; they may not be violated with impunity. This was for me nicely suggested in a contemporary introduction to one of Shakespeare's plays: "For example, a sympathetic, or simply pathetic, Sir Andrew [Aguecheek] presupposes a Sir Toby whose dark, rascally side must be exposed to the audiences long before his repudiation of his fellow-knight. Constraint in itself is not enough; a tomboyish Viola, who enjoys scrapping with Olivia's attendants, does not sort well with a mournfully infatuated Olivia."[6] These observations are useful reminders that, for the sake of such integrity as may characterize any life, credibility demands limitations. For Olivia's infatuation to be theatrically believable dictates only limited modes of Viola/Cesario's self-presentation. Similarly, there is no way that the enlargement of one's self-presentation can avoid arousing displeasure in those previously aware only of one's "best self." Ingredients of any given whole must be consistent with each other in the designated context.

The fifth of morning's attitudes may be rather closely related to its predecessor. Perhaps the *tendency to conceal one's uncertainties* is but one aspect of presenting only the "best" self. Out of the excruciating uncertainties of late adolescence we learned to act as though some things were true.

In the modern world it is impossible for a child to grow up without gradually becoming aware that there are no absolutes. It is no more possible to protect a child from this knowledge than it was long ago for Prince Gotama's father to keep him ignorant of the reality of suffering and death. By our student days it is impossible not to realize that it is only by an arbitrariness that a certain reality appears to be absolute. Whether or not that which so appears is absolute, we simply cannot know. The question undergraduates want (and need) to address to their teachers is this: "When it doesn't matter what, if anything, one does in the world, how do you justify the ways in which you spend time and energy?" An utterly legitimate and sometimes desperate question, it is probably just as well that it is not often asked. Most adults, certainly those still in life's morning, do not have the foggiest idea how they carried off such intellectual sleight of hand. They know only to rush youth on from adolescent and young adult relativism into all those commitments inherent in what we call "adulthood."

All young adults emerge, inasmuch as they do, from immobilizing (intellectual) uncertainties by making several basic commitments. The choice of work, spouse, values, all involve differing degrees of arbitrariness—there is no other way out of the immobility of indecision. Thus it is tempting in life's morning to pretend an excessive certitude. This seems to be especially widespread currently. Many men and women today hold political, religious and educational views apparently free of uncertainty. It is probable that this is a typical reaction following an era of relativism such as characterized the 1960s and 1970s. However, this pretense of certainty is deficient in two basic ways: it is at odds with the understandings to which more thoughtful people come, and it precludes the possibility of give-and-take by which such people arrive at the relative certainty that is the best of which we are capable.

Thus, in such an era as the present the social ethos strongly supports that which I am identifying as one of the attitudes appropriate to life's morning. There will be a temptation to insist for longer than might otherwise be necessary, on the certainty of one's particular convictions. Thus will be delayed the relaxation of such ideologies appropriate to the attitudes in life's afternoon. One of the features of graceful aging is the gradual abandonment of the pretense of certainty in favor of the ability to voice strong convictions about matters primarily affecting the shape of the future. For another of the important attitudes of one's later years is concern about the future as much as about the present, which tends to be the exclusive preoccupation of those in life's morning. Especially for those who are tempted to accuse older people of being preoccupied with the past, a pathology all too common among the aged, I contend that the normative interest for people in life's afternoon is a care for the emerging world.

It is this concern for society's future, in tandem with their lack of need for the pretended certainties of adults, that accounts for the mutual attraction between youth and older people. Positively, they experience much in common, such as having limited funds and employment, enjoying being with their own age group, and recognizing the extent to which they are "outsiders." Negatively, they have a common adversary in those who are most resolutely still in life's morning. So-called adults are rarely comfortable with either youth or old people: the former have not been adequately indoctrinated and are unsure of themselves; the latter seem to have moved beyond doctrine without becoming directionless. Both are a bafflement!

The last of morning's attributes of which I speak, again, may be but a variant on the preference of a part to the whole. At least the *preference for the will over the imagination* represents an imbalance, a rejection of the more difficult God-given wholeness. The assumption, nowhere seeming more clear than in the work of the United States Corps of Engineers, is that there are no obstacles that the combination of human skills and tenacity cannot overcome. The emphasis often seems to be on tenacity. Kindred to the mentality of the Corps are those who determine to build, irrespective of the fundamental geological facts of a chosen site. They remind one of the willful dean in William Golding's novel, *The Spire*, who was determined to erect the tallest tower in England despite the lack of bedrock. The arrogant willfulness which underlay his lack of architectural imagination is at least as well known now as then.

Whether or not the Strategic Defense Initiative is a contemporary example is a matter of disagreement among some authorities. In my mind it represents two dramatic deficiencies: a diminished imagination about diplomatic and other possibilities for negotiated peace and a willfulness that cannot but be grounded in both ineradicable fear of an enemy and an apocalyptic yearning for absolute security. Having no taste for the relative solutions of which imaginative negotiation is possible, some persons reach ruefully for absolutes that lie beyond human capability. In the political realm, especially in the international theater, this preference for the super-human over the merely human may be the most dangerous penchant of our time. It represents an intolerance of the only resources we possess for dealing with conflicts at all levels, from the domestic to the international. Distaste for the possible is the reality underlying this Faustian tragedy.

What I am calling imagination, which contrasts sharply with willfulness, includes *a deep appreciation for what is possible in the world.* Imagination can be distinguished from fantasy in that fantasy is a reaching for the impossible. Fantasy is inclined to scorn things that are merely possible; it desires to transcend human limitations. Coupled with willfulness, which I find characteristic of our times, it is the inability to accept the reality of limitations. Imagination, however, offers solution-seeking alternatives to all dreamed-for panaceas.

The trouble with life's morning is that the agenda has been preset by the society and there is no room for imaginative alternatives. Young people are not encouraged to seek a good "fit" between their inclinations and the possibilities for self-maintenance. Rather, however unavoidably ill-defined the concept, youth is told that the meaning of life lies only in the pursuit of success. Willpower seems to promise the ability to achieve those goals which we have been told to pursue. Whether or not they are right for each person, they are the prescribed desiderata and, like Pavlovian dogs, youth and the not-so-young pursue them with willful alacrity.

It should not surprise us that after twenty or so years of such effort many people acknowledge a fatigue which seems to arise from boredom. What else may we expect from an approach to the world that is deficient on at least two basic counts? First, the uniform goals that are offered ignore the rich variety of woman- and manhood produced in the society. Second, by insisting that all behave like women and men in gray flannel suits, it assures that there will be a number of people whose inner life never connects with the outer world in which they are urged to be productively busy. These conditions assure boredom, which is never possible when that connection is made; fatigue follows as the result of energy wasted in an effort to conceal boredom. The capacity of the will to sustain effort, even meaningless work, is determined by the extent to which the imagination can suggest possible connections between one's inwardness and the world one would influence by one's efforts. Ignorant of such fundamental human limitations—indeed blinded by a societal idolatry of the will, which is assumed to be able to do whatever the self desires—we overburden the will early and late. Childhood years signal only the beginning of programs in which we are asked to assent to endless self-improvement. As threateningly evidenced by programs such as Elderhostel, the process never ends. Nothing is ever allowed to lie fallow.

Such attitudes are notoriously lacking in imagination. Using images derived from inorganic surroundings rather than from organisms akin to the human, society attaches absolute importance to the will and remains ignorant of what beyond exhortation may be required to sustain the will's effectiveness. All popular opinion to the contrary notwithstanding, humans are not able to will whatever they can think of. People have great, but not limitless, resources of will, and it is the work of human imagination to determine when and where those finite resources may best be applied. The alternative is the bored fatigue with which some people conclude the work of life's morning. That many such are already deeply involved in self-destructive escapes should surprise no one. Fundamental conditions of viable life have been violated. Those who cannot long subscribe to society's lures, or pretend to do so, comfort themselves as best they can for their "failure." Such boredom or fatigue may provide incentive for some people to escape destructive pretense in favor of the more imaginative (*not* fantasy-filled!) work of life's afternoon.

THE MORNING IN PERSPECTIVE

These, then, are some of the major attributes of life-before-noon: an emphasis on the external, rather than internal, achievements; an assumed control to shape the future; various ways in which parts of the self are preferred to one's wholeness as a person; and an unrelieved confidence in the human will. It is important to be aware of these and any other characteristics of life during those decades; more important, however, is a clear understanding of the distinctiveness of that particular period of life.

There are several ideas here that require emphasis. First, because what we are calling the "morning" is the period when greatest effort is made and power acquired, there is a tendency to absolutize the virtues of this stage of life. This may be an exquisite illustration of the effort to make a part substitute for the whole, but it is no less perilous for that reason. Neither children nor elderly people, for example, are as interested in productivity, or even control, as are those in the decades of "adulthood." Yet those in that long and influential period between youth and age tend to insist that people's preoccupations and efforts are deficient to the extent that they are different from the agenda of life's morning. Thus, for all their usual lack of religious rationale, those living in the morning are subject to a much more serious idolatry than the making of images of God. *They presume that there is but one form of the human and that this norm is embodied in the successful adulthood of men and women of our time and place.* Were the presumption not so hurtful, both to adults and to those younger and older, we might be able to laugh at it. Perhaps because laughter is marginal to such "adulthood," rarely is amusement at its pretensions easily evoked.

Such idolatry makes impossible the important work of self-reclamation. Childhood is valued as the time of prefiguration for adulthood, old age justified by its preretirement productivity. Like leisure, the instrumental rationale for which is its ability to enable one to return to work, there are other periods of life that have no merit of their own. They are judged adequate or deficient as they support the productive virtues of life's morning. In the eyes of some, to lose one's interests as a consumer of goods is tantamount to being dead. That such loss might be the beginning of real life is incomprehensible. More seriously, by emphasizing the importance of the pursuit of societally identified goals this value neglects the self-acquaintance which is the precondition of reclamation. Reflection is discouraged, as is all questioning of societal goals where the latter is not actually prohibited. Like all ideology, which inflates the importance of aspects of reality, so the absolutizing of adulthood's virtues penalizes those of appropriate age whose thoughts and needs are at variance with prescribed norms. It is the all-too-familiar effort to make a part—and in this case a large and important part—serve as the whole. But because there is more to humanity than producing and consuming, the qualities that contribute to those ends are but part of life's needs. To the extent that they inhibit the formation of skills for life's later years they reveal the demonic potential in even the best of virtues.

My second demurrer can be simply stated: because of their contributions to modern life, there is a tendency to view morning's attributes as reality itself rather than as constructs that characterize a society. To the extent that this view is uncritically held we have an illustration of parochialism among those who mistakenly pride themselves on having taken the larger perspective.

Third, the idolatry of morning's agenda inhibits the development of the ingredients of some people's undeniable experience: for some—Emily Dickinson comes to mind—the nurture and expression of the inner life is a nonnegotiable imperative; for others—all those who become addicted to substances may illustrate—the presumed ability to control is found wanting; for still others the burden of pretense—of concealing one's imperfection—becomes unbearable. For all of these the need for reclamation is imperative, whatever their chronological age and whatever the cost in societal disapproval. For most people the need will become apparent only as there is progressive diminishment of adulthood's satisfactions. The task is so to fashion social life that whenever the work of reclaiming one's life becomes urgent there will be support for that hard work. Whether or not a society uncritically committed to activism can reach that level of maturity is as yet unproven.

The case has often been made for the religious character of the preoccupations of life's morning; however, I find myself at odds with that argument. That "case" is grounded in the conviction that it is good to sustain the world, with some kind of affirmation of the goodness of God's creation as given in Genesis 1:31. I am neither so audacious nor so depressed as to want to refute that rudimentary text on which so much of Western society stands. What I do feel the need to underscore, as probably every generation has recognized, is that the affirmation about the world's goodness routinely gets distorted. The forward thrust, which is inherent in the stewardly obligation to maintain the creation, routinely comes to be thought of as an end in itself. As this happens the human aptitudes that complement those intrinsic to the morning's work begin to be devalued. From devaluation the process leads inevitably to neglect, suspicion, and hostility. It is my clear impression that as a society, we are at least suspicious if not hostile to the work of critical reflection which I believe to be intrinsic both to life's afternoon and to a prophetic Christian faith.

The priestly role endures, of course; but it becomes accomplice to idolatry if divorced from that of the prophet who is always at least suspicious of societal goals and stances. Unavoidably, the prophet is the person burdened with the realization that every "arrangement" is to only some people's advantage. Others, for whom the prophet has not lost concern in the self-congratulations of every social achievement, are disadvantaged by the prevailing order of things. In the context of our present discussion, it is the prophet's vocation to see to it that those qualities necessary to life's afternoon continue to be honored and nurtured. Indeed, the very fact that there is something in addition to life's morning is central to the prophet's continuing message.

It is for whole lives that we are made in God's image. It is from the complexities of that wholeness, that we endlessly flee. To be exclusively interested in the morning's agenda is today's popular escape route. Such perpetual flight is a way of understanding what scripture means by sin. It is to sin so understood—in both its social and individual manifestations—that the prophet calls attention. That God may continue to see creation as "good," we must be urged, as we grow older, to affirm the agenda of life's afternoon with the vigor once limited to the morning's work.

Chapter 4

Unclaimed Lives

The late Dag Hammarskjöld kept a journal over the decades of his adult life. Until shortly before a fatal plane crash in 1961, while on a mission as Secretary General of the United Nations, he made irregular entries in what he called his *Markings*.[1] Although he was a person of deep faith and widely acknowledged success, Hammarskjöld lived with despair much of the time. For example, it was his custom to make the first entry of each new year a particular line from a hymn that his mother had customarily read to the family on New Year's Eve: "How vain the worldling's pomp and show . . . the night approaches now." For years his meditations on this set text reflected his melancholy, for example: "The night approaches now . . . and if this day should be your last . . ." or "The night approaches . . . how long the road is."

Eight years before his death, however, he recorded an utterly different response to the familiar words:

> The night approaches now—
> For all that has been—thanks!
> To all that shall be—yes!

Hope, which sustained him for the rest of his life, had been born.

Two persistent questions underlie our present discussion: How might we be helped to a comparable thankfulness? What is the process by which we both recognize and affirm as from God "all that has been"? It is the second of these with which

we shall be concerned here, for gratitude eventually arises
from a persistent effort to recognize what has been our experience. Disgust and despair are inseparable from the process,
but I am convinced with Hammerskjöld that they are not the
last word. Ultimately, we all must relinquish our lives. That
will be made easier the better acquainted we are with what
our life has been. That we may more gracefully relinquish our
lives finally is a secondary (and probably debatable) benefit of
learning to affirm "all that has been." The primary gain—a
wonderful paradox—is that the more we reconnect with our
past, the more vividly alive we are to the present and future.
By undertaking thus to gather ourselves together we may also
begin to reverse the fragmentation of lives so characteristic of
these times.

Beneath life's obvious changes, many of which are inescapable, lie each person's "givens," the genetic inheritance and
the time and place into which he or she is born. Heredity and
environment constitute the unchangeable warp. These are the
determining strands upon which experience accumulates.
When such experience is integrated, it becomes the recognizable weft of a person's life. The "fabric," the pattern of a person's
life, combines warp and weft. Although it has been accumulating at least since birth, and put to somewhat different uses
over life's stages, experience itself is not readily grasped.
Indeed, it is never fully understood. Its ultimate incomprehen-
sibility should, however, blind us neither to the gains inherent
in the process of reclaiming more of our experience nor to the
challenges of the task. (As in so many of his insights, Paul
describes succinctly the transcendent experience he expects:
"The knowledge that I have now is imperfect; but then I shall
know fully as I am known" [1 Corinthians 13:12, JB]). In the
meantime, of course, we see through a glass darkly.

MAKING SENSE OF EXPERIENCE

Everybody has myriad experiences—day and night, summer
and winter, childhood and age, victories and defeats, pleasures
and pains, conflict and reconciliation. All these and many more
are constantly intermingling within and around us. Awake or

asleep, we are constantly bombarded by the raw data of experience. Regrettably, most people acknowledge only a limited relationship to all that has happened to them. Yet they seek wider vistas—for example, through travel or new relationships—as though more experience might satisfy the deep yearning to make more sense of their lives. They fail to see that "more" is not the answer. If we are to see more clearly through the dark glass, what we need is a more intentional relationship to what has transpired over the decades. At the least, we must begin to acknowledge personal relationship to what may have been the major threads of our lives. It is the *drift* of our life—its "inscape" as well as landscape—with which we need to become acquainted. Thus would we begin to claim as our own, shiny or shabby—and all lives are something of both—the experiences in which lie some of the meaning we seek. The result will not be all gain; there are illusions to abandon. Both they and their abandonment, and our reasons for affirming or discarding them, will be important dimensions of our experience. Shedding these will not be just like anybody else's experience, however alike we largely are, especially in the illusions to which we subscribe. What it will be is partial, sometimes hopeful, often frustrating, but ours! We will have begun to lay claim to the one and only life that is assuredly our own.

To urge this important work is not to be blind to its inherent difficulties. In many ways the task is something like that which confronts the historian. "Out there" is a mountain of data—artifacts, sites, public documents, individual recollections—which will not organize itself. It just *was*: lived history, placid or turbulent. To make sense of at least parts of it, the historian must have a perspective from which to sift the sources and, on the basis of that outlook, to identify some things as important, others not so. No two historians will read the data in exactly the same way, though all may contribute to understanding the past. It is not until such digging and sifting has been done by others that one is able both to know what happened and to determine how to relate to the historians' reports. Thus do we acknowledge the importance of recalled

events or persons for both our self-understanding and our
national identity.

The PBS television series "Eyes on the Prize: America's Civil
Rights Years, 1954–1965" is a superb illustration of an era of
conflict to which no citizen has the right to be indifferent.
Events occurred, events often almost incomprehensibly violent
from our present perspective, by which all lives were changed.
Although the impact of these changes on people's lives was
anything but uniform, I doubt that anybody's self-understanding has remained what it was in the decades when Jim Crow
was the "law" of at least part of the land. Nor does certain
once-condoned behavior enjoy quite the community support by
which it was earlier sustained. Many paid heavy prices to
effect these changes. Ignorance about this history may be but
a means of refusing to acknowledge relationship to these
events. Thus may ignorance be an accomplice of the deeper
aversion to internal change.

To lay claim to one's life involves making some sense out of
a mound of data similar to that which confronts the historian.
Furthermore, a person's vast experience may be no more self-
explanatory or self-organizing than are the historian's materials. Our data are, however, largely internal, hidden somewhere in our memories. (As the series "Eyes on the Prize"
reminds us, personal recollections are rarely purely subjective.
Our deep reservoir of experience almost always relates to
encounters with something in the world outside.) To gain
access to the raw materials of one's own life—the experience
that one alone has had, however much stimulated by public
events—requires a perspective to assist in the winnowing and
sifting process. No less important than it is for the historian,
and no more easily identified as our working tool, we need to
discover what our deep perspective really is in order to claim
accurately the responsibility for the life we have actually lived.
Just as there is much inaccurate recording of history, so is
faulty self-reporting a possibility. Although no perspective
assures absolute accuracy, what we are able to identify and
claim of our experience must be as truthful as possible. Inasmuch as it is the valuable lode hidden in our experience that

we hope to reclaim, it is imperative to avoid those perspectives that would yield fewer riches.

Even so, misrepresentation is as unavoidable in individual recollection as in the historian's work. We must always have a perspective which makes it possible to make *some* sense out of material with which we must deal. Even to be able to arrange that material chronologically, which is often a helpful start, is not necessarily to arrange it properly in terms of its significance. It will *not* arrange itself, and there is always something inescapably arbitrary about any perspective we employ. However inclusive we would be, every perspective at once reveals and conceals. It is for this purely academic reason that we may be able to see the need for both neighbor and God. Lines from Robert Burns point to the former: "Give us the grace to see ourselves as others see us." Our biographers would not write about us as we might compose our autobiography. Both perspectives are necessary for anything approaching a complete portrait. Even so, much about us remains hidden from others and from ourselves. As Paul recognized, until time's end, we "see in a mirror dimly" (1 Corinthians 13:12). Whatever a person's faith stance, that insight should be universally affirmable. Paul's insistence that God is our final biographer may not be equally to the liking of all: Christians are fortunate in the belief that God is merciful. That the God who knows all may forgive all is *the* good news. (Forgiveness among neighbors cannot stem from such comprehensive knowledge. What is true for the Creator is *not* true for God's creatures. For us the order is reversed: to be forgiven is to be capable of knowing/seeing more than otherwise.)

In the meantime, and as we move toward such self-comprehensiveness, we shall employ a succession of perspectives. In the final analysis, however, we shall be made whole by grace rather than by the completeness of our recollections. No perspective will be salvific.

Since such a recognition is central to the work of self-reclamation, we can recognize why the presence of older people in church and synagogue is so appropriate. Much more than youth, who expect to fashion their own lives, and unlike adults in the middle years, who harbor the illusion that they have a perspective on their lives that will make them self-justifying, older people have come to several potentially devastating realizations. Through experience they know youthful vision and adult invulnerability to be illusory. Nobody fashions a life alone, nor do anybody's accomplishments, however great, fully protect against loss and despair. More important than either of these, but a consequence of them, older people are coming to realize that God is their biographer. It is through God's eyes that every life will be read. Youth and adults have yet to discover this truth.

That God is our final biographer does not invalidate the work of self-reclamation. Only as that work progresses, as we move to an ever more adequate perspective for data sifting and evaluation, does it become apparent that total reclamation eludes us. This is another, perhaps the last, instance in which despair threatens to overwhelm us. We cannot even tell our own story completely. J. B. Phillips's translation of one of Paul's sentences indicates the apostle's awareness of the incompleteness of his self-knowledge and that this need not occasion despair. "At present all I know is a little fraction of the truth, but the time will come when I shall know it as fully as God now knows me" (1 Corinthians 13:12, Phillips). That the God who now knows fully is gracious warrants patience about a coming time when we shall know ourselves fully.

We shall give careful attention later to a discussion of what is for me the perspective needed for the work of laying claim accurately to our experience. How much justice we can do to the diversity of experience—its highs and its lows—without affirming our ultimate grounding in the image of God is one of the questions we shall have to address. For both the historian in public work and the individual in search of self-understanding, perspective determines what we can "see" and, even more important, how able we are to claim as our own whatever we may discover to have been true in our experience. At many points the *courage* to acknowledge what one has found is *the* issue. Historians and self-historians are often tempted to bury information that is at apparent odds with prior understandings. It is not easy to present oneself or one's society "warts and all." Successful concealment is, however, inimical to both endeavors.

We need to undertake the difficult assignment of rediscovering our experience *and* claiming it as our own. It is a work involving both learning about and embracing the import of the new knowledge for one's self-understanding. A measure of pretense will probably endure to the end of life, but it can gradually yield to more accurate self-acquaintance. Recognition of these coordinate assignments of intellect *and* character—to discover what has been true of one's life and to have the courage to embrace what one has found—may be the point at which to emphasize that competence alone is not enough. Were that the case, there would be no need to include the Christian gospel in the discussion. If learning alone assured reclamation, the task would be much simpler. Unfortunately, no such assurance is possible.

FORGIVENESS THE WAY TO KNOWLEDGE

In my understanding, and contrary to an ancient maxim, it is not true that to know all is to forgive all. No quantity of knowledge, however vast, ever takes one to forgiveness. There is nothing in learning as such that makes one forgiving either of others or of oneself. Indeed, it is often the case that the more learned some persons are, the more impatient they are with others' shortcomings and the more gifted in concealing their own. (Alternatively, learning may prompt some persons to inflate their shortcomings on the assumption that it is better to be notorious than merely mediocre.)

It all works, I suspect, just the opposite of what the academy advertises. It is by being forgiven that we receive seeing eyes and hearing ears. These are neither natural capabilities nor acquired skills. Rather than assuming that the greater one's knowledge, the greater is one's ability to forgive, to the point where to know all is to forgive all, I suggest that the knowledge of being forgiven determines how much about our own lives we shall have the competence to see and the courage to claim. This is especially the case when we seek to come to terms with our personal story. Here, where it is virtually impossible ever to be objective, our natural discernment will never present an accurate picture of who we are. The potential for misrepresenting ourselves is endless. (Although it takes us beyond our present discussion, the need for forgiveness is relevant to what we call *personal* history especially as we recognize that our personal story is inseparable from several larger contexts. The import of such factors as sex, race, class, and nationality, to our self-understanding means that they are matters for which forgiving eyes are more important than we realize.) The gains in reclaiming one's life are immeasurable.

To refuse this task is no casual matter. Rather than having access at least to the riches inherent in our past, we draw on an ever-diminishing range of experience. For example, rather than being capable of varied responses appropriate to similar but not identical situations, we have predictable reactions which ignore the differences. Rather than being capable of an ever-larger range of harmonies and dissonances, we can play ever-fewer tunes. In extreme instances of mental illness, a person may have but a single theme, endlessly repeated. Having claimed only a limited range of experience and using this as the perspective by which all else is judged, the person is prisoner in a self-fashioned confinement. Escape from such imprisonment, to which in varying degrees all are subject, is possible only by being able to lay claim to more of our experience. Repetition of the single theme, however increased the volume, will never accomplish a jailbreak: the louder the sound, the more binding the entrapment. The long-repeated record must be changed, even if only played at a different speed, by recognizing that there has been more to us than we have been able to see. At that moment the confining chains begin to loosen. By claiming ever more of our previously unclaimed lives we begin the escape to freedom.

It is difficult to imagine a circumstance in which it is not vital to be able to say, "Thank God, there's more to me than that!" The confinements we experience are as often parts of others' attempts to constrict us as they are self-imposed. Others often want to limit us to roles with which they are comfortable. Frequently we find it appropriate and comfortable to stay within those confines. Occasionally, though, it is imperative that we be able to escape such roles. To do this, to have the necessary courage, requires knowledge that there has been and is much more to us than can ever fit into any particular mold. This was nicely illustrated during the second episode of "Eyes on the Prize" which dealt with some of the events of 1961. As the first of the Freedom Riders made their way into the deeper South, the question facing the governor of Alabama was whether or not the state would assure the safe passage of that small group of black and white men and women. Clearly reluctant to provide such assurance for the "agitators," even in response to direct pressure from the federal attorney general's office, the impasse was at least momentarily resolved by the chief of Alabama's highway patrol. A mild-mannered native Alabaman, Colonel Mann assured the state's officials that it was within the capability of his staff to provide such public safety. It was not made clear in the program how unanticipated—or unwelcome—was his initiative but, clearly, he spoke in quite a different voice from that of the governor. For whatever reasons, Colonel Mann spoke on that occasion in response to some imperative that would not allow him to hide within the role expected of him.

We are not automata with completely predictable behavior. Although we ordinarily act more or less predictably, thereby giving appropriate assurance to others that we are much the person today that they knew yesterday, there is always something more than the predictable, and at least as important, to our deeper identity. We all are men and women of considerable experience, however limited our travel or range of acquaintances, and capable of acting with some freedom. Coupled with the reassurance to others of the ordinary continuity of our lives there is an endless potential for thinking and acting in fresh ways. This potential for unfamiliar behavior may be unsettling to others, as I suspect it was that day to those in Alabama Governor Morrison's office, and even to ourselves at times. Discontinuity is, however, the other key to our humanity, and it is nurtured from the depths of our varied experience.

The less aware of this we are, the more predictable our behavior; the more in touch with our experience we are, the greater our potential for creativity. We do not need to react as we long have to a familiar provocation; we have the potential for viewing it in a somewhat different light. The balance of continuity and discontinuity in our lives will never be resolved to everybody's complete satisfaction. Surprises will be tolerable only to the extent that they are the occasional behavior of ordinarily reliable people. The enduring need, however, is not for ever-greater support for continuity; rather, it is for assurance that ample encouragement is given to the universal potential for, and the occasional urgent need of, that freedom which makes us distinctively human. It is this, rather than the capacity for conformity, which society is most often tempted to curtail. As we insisted in the last chapter, the inclination to absolutize the agenda of life's morning, to insist that the emphases then appropriate remain the criteria for people at all stages, is ill advised. Older people, responding to distinctive inner promptings, need to be free to get about their somewhat different business. In certain ways, and with varying intensity among individuals, aging calls for some measure of discontinuity.

Two months after writing this paragraph, I had a traumatic experience which may modify slightly the importance I give to discontinuity. I still do not believe that the balance between continuity and discontinuity will ever be settled to everybody's satisfaction, but I understand better many people's aversion to discontinuity.

What happened quite suddenly was a near-fatal abdominal sickness. Although the pain during the twenty-four hours required for diagnosis was unlike anything I had ever experienced, that was not the discontinuity from which I found myself wanting to escape. Actually that pain ceased with the surgery which removed an infected portion of colon. Nor were the procedures of the postsurgical days—the tubes, the odd routines of hospital life—among the discontinuities I dreaded. Most of the devices I disliked but accepted as temporarily necessary. Gradually, as I improved, they were removed until finally I had nothing strange entering or leaving my body. That was a good feeling: I was once again myself.

Or was I? Would I ever be what I had been on the day that pain had driven me to dial the emergency number? These were questions arising from discontinuity which might not be dismissible. For at least two reasons they seemed to be enduring: first, my personal "plumbing" had been irreversibly changed and, second, I had received a compelling reminder of my mortality. For at least these reasons I was aware of life's discontinuity, and—this is a point I need to emphasize—I was not keen on them!

Vastly more important than my slightly modified viscera was the vivid reminder of my mortality. This, about which most of us think as little as possible, is the extreme of discontinuity. Beyond the need for a modified diet was the lurking realization that there might soon be a time—had recently almost been a time—when I would not eat again. Other things came to mind, all of the wonderful—sensual, intellectual, emotional—experiences that go into the making of our inspirited lives. All these were somewhat imperiled, and I was *unwilling* to dwell on that possibility. For all of my earlier emphasis on the importance of discontinuity, which I will not rescind, when the realities came to me as life or death possibilities I found myself to be on the continuity side!

Rather than pondering regularly the existential import of the fact that I would not live forever, as we all *know* intellectually (which hardly addresses the reality), I was grateful for every hurdle cleared on the way back to my life as it had been. I was again able to enjoy food, engage in regular activities, and reaffirm relationships. I cherished the recovery of the simple things, for example, having been a jogger for two decades, I rejoiced that I could run fifty feet! A small achievement, to be sure, but a thread in the pattern of continuity which I coveted. In the long run such matters have something less than absolute importance. In the context of a discontinuity that I knew would persist, however, I found these modest gains reassuring. That is the discovery which seems important to share in light of views expressed above prior to an instructive traumatic experience.

CLAIMING OUR LIVES

With this understanding of the enduring tension between the need for both continuity and discontinuity throughout life, the task we shall address here may be stated simply: we seek both to recognize the extent to which our lives are unclaimed and to become aware of how unfortunate—should I say dangerous? tragic?—is such alienation.

For most people a time arrives when the effects of their unclaimed lives become progressively clear. We have all made many decisions over the decades without giving much thought to their long-range consequences. We proceeded into major areas of human activity, such as work and significant relationships, at least as ignorant as we were informed about what to expect eventually. For the most part we failed to anticipate the power of the combination of partial intentionality, ignorance, and the passage of time to influence our ability to continue to affirm commitments. Lacking sufficient self-understanding in youth and young adulthood—and such may not be within one's capability at that age—we made choices for which we sometimes later discovered that we lacked heart. Underlying these realities was the failure to wonder about the depths of faith at which lives may need to be grounded. Such unclaimed experience often leads to what is popularly referred to as "mid-life crisis." The need for claiming our experience may also lead us to a fresh understanding of Christian faith. For if that faith means anything, it has to do with the need to be in touch with our experience.

My thesis is that the extent to which a person's experience is claimable is directly proportionate to the depth at which that life is grounded. Perhaps only by a life rooted in the mystery of the God to whom both Judaism and Christianity point is it possible to claim as our own the myriad experiences of one's life. This work is not just a matter of knowledge. It requires a sense of identity sufficient to yield the courage to assent to what we would otherwise choose to ignore. In each of the major areas of human experience, there are ultimate questions. It is this fact that validates them as spheres of human activity. If we are indifferent to the lingering presence of such questions, we will be oblivious to the gracious Presence in which everything inheres.

All the areas of human experience have some validity in themselves. Given also the need for some firm grounding for our lives, we are tempted to exaggerate the importance of one or more of them. Although other societies, and our own at times, have emphasized varied facets of experience, such as knowledge, physical beauty, or *machismo*, the importance of work is currently inflated. To the extent that we do this we ask more meaning from an aspect of human experience than it is able to yield. This is idolatry: the attempt to absolutize a relatively valuable area of experience. Ubiquitous and unending, the temptation to overburden work as a source of meaning is based on a promise incapable of providing the desired fulfillment. In response to disillusionment following overinvestment in one activity it is common for people to transfer hope to another seemingly more promising endeavor. There may well be no alternative to such "shopping." Perhaps fatigue is part of the divine pedagogy to enable us to discover that only in God can we hope to invest ourselves usefully in various activities without needing to absolutize any one of them.

Having stressed the importance of reclaiming one's life, it is imperative to be clear about the significance of that for the development of a mature Christian faith. The former does not assure the latter. Whether or not one becomes a person of genuine faith is not the result of effort, however heroic. That remains a gift of grace.

Why, then, do I urge the painful work of self-reclamation? Why not leave myself to God's grace in all my ignorance? Because I have not found that it works that way. Preparation, which is how I view the work of reclamation, is inseparable from the process of receiving grace. Preparation does not determine faith, but the latter does not ordinarily occur apart from the former. Patience, a requirement which is resented in an "instant" society, is an intrinsic ingredient of the preparation process. Contrary to prevailing assumptions that things must occur immediately, or at least on schedule, the person seeking faith must learn both to work at the preparatory tasks and to wait. It is not God who does the waiting.

The way out of this frustration requires us to change our understandings of the routes toward mature faith. We must go beyond the two paths which William James described in his epochal study, *The Varieties of Religious Experience*. However enduringly valuable that work remains, James limits his discussion to only two types of religious experience: those of the "once born" and of the "twice born." There are those who seem to imbibe faith in infancy and proceed through life with but minor redirections. The twice born are those "born again," who experience traumatic upheavals on the abrupt road to faith. Paul was one such and there are many contemporaries who profess such experience.

The problem is that although there remain men and women whose experience fits into one or the other Jamesian category, neither describes a route of which many late-twentieth-century people are capable. His varieties fail to provide for the distinctive experiences of such people. Their childhood faith was early eroded, if not dashed in some particular instances, by discovering the varied lives people in our society actually lead. Relativism does not support the comparatively sanguine faith of the "once born." Some of these people will be candidates for dramatic. rebirth, but such instantaneous reversal will not be the route for the majority. Radical redirection of a life should never be the norm by which all other experience is to be judged. It happens, to be sure, but this position is never easy to sustain. The level of recidivism is predictably high.

For the majority, the more gradual process will involve stages of faith in which the preparations of a particular stage will, by grace, be incorporated into an ever-more integrated life. Such men and women will experience neither the continuity of the "once born" nor the discontinuity of those radically reborn. Their process of multiple rebirths will be lifelong and never free of trauma. There will be changes in the process of reclaiming our experience and discovering that God accepts us even in spite of what we have discovered about ourselves. We become acceptable to God only in relation to our efforts at self-reclamation. The process is unending, for God only becomes God for us, the One who accepts our efforts and imbues us with courage for the next task, in connection with our efforts to reclaim more of our actual lives. It is only in the light of lives so affirmed/acknowledged, lives which we feared nobody could love, that God may become God for us. These steps signal the end of all "best-self"-only religion. It is not the effort at self-reclamation that saves us. Rather, that we try indicates that we understand the importance of our life in time and that we honor the gift of memory as the means of reversing the fragmentation of the image of God in which we are made.

Despite its blatant inadequacies such religion of the "best self" will not readily yield to any alternative. It is too deeply rooted in the lives of the self-righteous, who constitute a majority of the once born, and who are too dependent on others' approval of them to be amenable to change, whether radical or gradual. The penchant for continuity may be the reason that certain societies resist all significant knowledge that may mandate change.

In today's world, and especially in areas to which modern media have almost constant access, it is difficult to see how such self-insulation will continue to be effective. Since long before the electronic age, people have been giving each other significant information more or less constantly. Even household pets pick up clues of approval and disapproval—many of these nonverbal—and modify their behavior accordingly. We have to be either resolutely arrogant or alarmingly obtuse not to pick up certain responses to our behavior from those with whom we live. Yet many seem deaf and blind to the information that those around them try to convey about the effects of their presence in the variety of day-to-day life situations.

Whether or not we pay attention to the situation depends, I believe, on our openness to grace. For grace is not (primarily) a matter of information. We cannot avoid the constant flow of data from our dealings with others. Cues are coming to us most of the time. The issue at hand is this: what am I *able to do* with that information? It is never possible simply to incorporate those cues in a new self-presentation; we cannot simply cease being what we have been in order to demonstrate our ability to hear others' opinions of us. Between that compliant response and the refusal to acknowledge others' views of us, however, there is a possible moment of grace. Without knowing fully the implications, we wish to incorporate in our lives some of the new knowledge that comes from human dialogue. Grace is evident when, rather than shunting such information aside, we willingly, if cautiously, embrace it.

SIGNS OF GRACE

Such new knowledge is unavoidable for all who live with others. It is part of what we are capable of generating for and learning from others by virtue of our God-given humanity. The crucial question is what we would like to make of what we have unavoidably learned. Because it involves change, which is always to a degree painful, some will want nothing to do with self-knowledge. Those who are willing to undertake the suffering of incorporating in their self-understanding new and not always congenial information give evidence of God's grace in their lives. Grace as such is without content. Its exclusive focus is on the positive incorporation of unsought knowledge in gradually changing lives. The process will happen many times, and persons of faith will not always assent to the direction in which God's grace would have them go. We may long be reluctant to admit certain information about ourselves. Faithful persons will even abandon the self-knowledge they have earlier internalized. The potential for apostasy is unending. Nevertheless, this need not permanently thwart the enlightenment toward which God endlessly lures us. The point is to avoid being too successfully resistant to those lures, too hard of heart.

The life of faith is, for increasing numbers of people as we approach the year 2000, more a lifelong *process* of maturation—including reverses and wrong directions over the entire course—than was envisioned at the turn of the present century by William James. The old certainties are gone. The opportu-

nity for maturing lives of faith is at hand for those who are
motivated to reclaim some parts of their lost lives and who
discover that even acquiring knowledge requires a depth of
grounding they had not anticipated. The possibility for despair
clearly inheres in this discovery. So, also, do recurrent steps in
grace.

Whether or not people can be persuaded to undertake the
difficult work of self-reclamation remains to be seen. In my
darker moments, I have my doubts that many will move
beyond the indulgence and self-deception of nostalgia. What
can be stated clearly is the *Christian* reasoning that underlies
my appeal to those who are progressively distanced from their
own actual lives. The rationale has two, intimately related,
primary sources: an understanding of God's nature and a
historical understanding of humanity's progressive alienation,
since the Renaissance, from all meaningful connections. The
process of distancing has, in our time, reached its nadir: late-
twentieth-century men and women are estranged not only from
nature, but also from their culture and hope itself. Perhaps
because of these broken connections we are detached from our
own lives. It has come to that. In my understanding of the
divine nature, it is possible for God to be known as gracious
only by people who struggle to discover some of these connections which are the sources of *meaningful* experience. The two
situations in which God cannot be so known are these: one,
when a person sees the meaning of his or her life to be quite
clear (confidence in self-justification, or ideological adequacy
precludes God's presence); two, when a person prefers any
diversion to the painful work of self-acquaintance. God may be
known as gracious, which is Christianity's ultimate word
("While we still were sinners Christ died for us" [Romans 5:8])
only when a person recognizes his or her need for grace. Other
aspects of God *may* be grasped under other circumstances, for
example, the evidence of the Creator/Sustainer may be discerned within the cosmos, but these are neither distinctively
Christian nor will they long satisfy persons who come to
wonder about the meaning of their particular lives. Neither
cosmological "evidence" nor convictions of moral rectitude are

adequate compensation for the sense of God's absence in response to one's existential plight.

Although there will be some passing references to the devo-
lution of the modern centuries, I will not attempt to document
that dehumanization here. Others have written such studies.[2]
What I intend, which may be more within my capability, is to
try to address as a Christian those readers who recognize in
their lives the alienation and emptiness which are the bitter
fruits of centuries of ever-increasing emphasis on "man as the
measure." Unfortunately, that emphasis needs to be understood as multiple disconnections from the basic relationships
within which our humanity lies. I do not intend a lament of
the technological excesses of our time, except as technological
surfeit may be a diversion acceptable to many who decline the
work of self-reclamation. (For example, some people delight in
"playing" with their computers.) Entertainment, which cannot
forever satisfy, surely is one of the demons of these times ready
to proclaim itself adequate to fill every emptiness in very
empty lives. What we must emphasize is that Western developments since the Renaissance have not made it easier to be in
touch with our own actual lives. So disconnected, we are ready
candidates for most diversions. That they do not long divert is
the painful discovery.

What we refer to as mid-life crisis is indeed a profound crisis
of faith: Can one continue to pursue with hope those activities
and relationships to which one has given oneself with vigor for
many years? Or, did illusions which must be confronted underlie that hope and those efforts? If the latter, what might
encourage one to undertake at least a partial dismantling of
such a life? The perils of the confrontations are undeniable.
What orientation might help to make sense of such risk taking?

These questions are really but oblique efforts to ask what
sense we make of life's middle and later years. Is aging an
absurd joke about which nothing is really funny? Or, as I
increasingly suspect, is it a good and necessary stage in which,
at some cost but with distinctive rewards, persons of Christian
faith will be able to let go of earlier illusions in favor of the

greater fruitfulness of their present lives? Critical to these illusions was the assumption that the life-task is to demonstrate the wisdom of the commitments made in early adulthood. These were rarely well-informed choices, and nobody could foresee their consequences with certainty, yet much was riding on their viability. Therefore, it seemed imperative to be able so to demonstrate their value. Such was their power to motivate significant effort that the commitments themselves could not be questioned. For a time, at least, they were absolutes the meaning of which both empowered us and sometimes rewarded our considerable efforts.

At some point questions about these commitments become irrepressible. Fatigue, coupled with an awareness of life's brevity and, most important, long-suppressed aspects of the self seeking recognition occasioned the inquiries. There is more to every one of us than fits comfortably into the packaged commitments of early adulthood. For varyingly long times people can act as though there is nothing more to them than the roles they choose to play. God help those who persist in that pretense to the end! Most yearn for larger, or more accurate, self-presentation. This is an important ingredient in the search for meaning which Jung said made the needs of mid-life patients essentially religious. Grateful for his sensitive humanism, we can assert that only the presence of God who is gracious is adequate to our needs at such a time of life. For our work in life's afternoon is to claim that which we largely ignored in the decades of attempted self-justification. What emerges from such work is often sufficiently unattractive to discourage the process unless we come to believe two important things. First, God will be gracious to those who are searching painfully for God's presence during years when they thought there was no reality but self and others. Second, as Augustine discovered, by the work of reclamation, for which God's presence frees us, the believer discovers that God has been present all the time. This discovery, many have said, is the pearl of great price for which all else may be sacrificed. Paradoxically, it is a genuine sacrifice in which nothing is lost.

Earlier I used an analogy to suggest the ingredients by

which lives are shaped. To the warp, one's distinctive "givens," life adds experience. The human task is to weave these additions, the weft, into what becomes one's personal fabric—something as distinctive as individual fingerprints. Most of us are neither consistent nor willing weavers. That the work is never easy means that much of the weft is ill-woven if not actually lost. The well-integrated life, like the well-made tapestry, is a precious rarity.

It is in the interest of reclaiming important lost threads and, where possible, reweaving a somewhat richer life that this book is written. Much experience in individual lives may be irrecoverably lost. However, given our reluctance to undertake the hard work, this may be less true than we often let ourselves believe. What is at least possible is to begin to identify our "givens" and, less easily, to discover how these contributed to our distinctive ways of self-investment. Do the "givens" of our lives, such as our genetic inheritance and the time and place of birth, contribute to our commitments to values? marriage? career? Or do they *determine* these commitments? At the least, they influence them. For all people at some times, the influence may seem determinative, which is how some people always experience their influence. Such decisions about our commitments will themselves not be easily reversed. Since they may have become central to our self-understanding, we may simply have to live with them as part of our reclaimed lives. Some will, however, be modifiable if we are willing to pay the price of such change. This, I suspect, is how it has always been, though different in degree for each of us. The key to any change is the ability to learn from our mistakes. The work of reclamation may just depend on something as simple and repugnant as that!

Chapter 5

Aging As Counterculture

Do we really believe that the positive views of previous societies about human aging were wrong? Have the changes of the past century, especially those of the decades since World War II, confirmed a long-standing American suspicion that age has nothing to teach? Has the New World's posture, long tipped toward the future, turned wholly in that direction? Are we free of all need to learn from the past? Are we confident that there is no wisdom either from antiquity or from our elderly contemporaries?

Questions like these, reflecting such negative attitudes, must have deep roots. Aversion to physical decrepitude, even to reminders of our mortality, does not account for our apparent determination to discard the positive attitudes of other cultures toward the elderly. Something more than youth-oriented attitudes must be adduced to account for the repugnance which many seem to have toward aging. Such deep feeling is involved that it is as though we had been frightened by something. Is it possible that our fright is rooted in the suspicion that the elderly may have grasped some important wisdom not accessible earlier in life? Would anything less than deeply threatening fear account for both the force and the extent of our ageism?

Before discussing further the possible roots of such powerful fear, we should note that ignorance may also be an important factor. We are apprehensive about old people and often put off by them because we seem not to realize that developments in human lives continue until death. This cannot be emphasized sufficiently. People do not achieve a certain stage of life that we call adulthood and then remain unchanged forever. Whether they intend it or not, and certainly independent of the graying of hair or need for eyeglasses, people's perspectives change. Growth is not inevitable, but as long as a person breathes further maturation is possible. This may be my most important thesis; certainly it is the most radical. It is based on the understandings advanced by contemporary students of human development. Only ignorance insists that at some point between cradle and grave life becomes unchanging. Public opinion and media emphases to the contrary, there is *no* ideal stage at which development may be stopped. Some periods in individual lives will seem preferable to others; the preferred era varies from person to person and may well change over a lifetime. The heartening fact in the context of our immediate discussion is that increasing numbers of people feel best about life's later years! Though it is often thwarted, important growth is always on the verge of happening. That some may regress is regrettable, but the possibility of change is a vital reminder of life's unending dynamic.

OUR UNENDING POTENTIAL FOR GROWTH

Whatever else may be involved in our deep aversion to aging, we must emphasize here the damage done by our failure to embrace the *unending* potential for growth. The potential for lives to continue to mature does not cease before physical death. However few or many people may reach that potential in no way influences our emphasis here: the growth of a human life does not stop at any chronological age. Physical maturation, which has no bearing on the maturity I have in mind, does cease early. As a society, we must move far beyond the assumption that no other changes ordinarily occur. In my understanding, physical maturity only establishes a comparatively stable base on which the only partly scripted drama of life may begin. For as long as we remain naive about the real-life theater of lives, somebody will have to protest such ignorance. That the aged have long been victimized by attitudes that deny the possibility of dramatic developments throughout life is but one of the reasons I have come to view aging as a countercultural force. Ignorance about changes in normal adult lives is a result of our inability to value either the variety of lives or the emphases distinctive to life's successive stages. There is simply no way that an adolescent and a mature adult in mid-life can see things similarly. Nor would an eighty-year-old agree completely with the understandings of that mature adult. Our crisis arises from the inability to value the achievements or to take seriously the perspectives of anybody other than those at mid-life maturity. We are ideologically deaf, dumb, and blind!

Awareness of this *potential* for further maturation underlies the more positive attitudes toward aging in other societies. To persist in our negative views of growing older is unwarranted and, in part, the result of willful ignorance. As things continue to happen over a lifetime, so people may continue to learn from their experience. Our fears about those who have grown old may stem in part from the suspicion they may have learned something which younger people are incapable of understanding. Some things are just not ordinarily graspable except as the result of experience in markedly extended lives. Time's passage is vastly more instructive than we acknowledge. Such, at least, is my suspicion and accounts for the title of this chapter, "Aging As Counterculture."

Older people may remind us of our mortality without engendering in us such a deep aversion to them. They may have more than their share of income, as some charge, and may require an inordinate percentage of the national health-care dollars, without moving us to ageist attitudes. We may fight them for a larger share of the economic pie without hating them.

What may frighten us about the elderly is their changing attitudes toward the prevailing way of life. The change may be as modest as a diminishing interest in the activities central to a consumer society. Depending on the depth of their original belief in the value of acquisitions, for example, they may simply be less interested in "shopping" than they once were. At the other extreme—again, perhaps reflecting the extent of their de-illusionment—they may insist on exposing the ephemeral nature of the lures by which they were once motivated to pursue success. With the passage of time, perspectives change. Why we refuse to embrace such a self-evident axiom is a societal mystery I seek to understand.

It is not the imminence of death that changes the attitudes of some of the elderly. Just the reverse is true. It is the older persons' unavoidably changing attitudes toward many of the pursuits they have long seemed to enjoy—pursuits often slow to disclose their inherent emptiness—which may trigger apprehensions about death. Although physical death is never accepted as the "natural" end for human beings in the sense it is for other forms of life, what is really unsettling is the gradual realization of how meaningless have been many of the things to which one gave much of one's life. The realization of a wasted life may be at least as traumatic as the prospect of a person's physical death. If this happens soon enough, there is yet time for the person to take a somewhat different direction for the balance of his or her life.[1] Discovery of the need for new direction does not usually come while a person is busy "keeping up with the neighbors." The eye is too keenly and exclusively focused on neighborhood values. It is only after many of the well-recommended targets have been achieved that a person begins to realize their illusory and/or transient nature.

Many who are younger may find this capability in the aging—to embody a counterculture—to be strongly objectionable. Yet, such potential ability to occupy "alien" ground may well be aging's vocation from God. Central to one's calling, of which many easily lose sight in those decades of pursuing success, is the awareness of *the relative nature* of all achievements and acquisitions. Without wanting to condemn all such pursuits, which are an intrinsic part of life in all societies, I emphasize only *the uniquely absolute character* of a person's relationship to God. That is the faith grounding, *the vocation*, to which expression must be given in one's life in the world. One's work is not one's vocation. At best it may be but one of the means by which one gives expression to one's calling. The problem is that in our society it is extremely difficult not to absolutize the work we do. Contrary to often-heard religious exhortations on behalf of vocational intensity, the extent of one's diligence in work is often a subtle indicator of how remote one has become from one's calling by God. For many people workaholism is the preferred alternative to faith. Their career becomes their god, with all of the perils inherent in absolutizing something of but relative importance.

As awareness of the possible meaningless of his or her work first dawns on a person, which often signals the onset of the trauma of mid-life, the initial reaction frequently is to apply greater effort. Since this prescription has often seemed to work earlier, many people double their diligence in the frantic hope of recovering lost satisfactions. Sometimes it does work, but rarely for very long. Through such an experience of loss, God is in the process of trying to instruct us. Since these lessons strike at the heart of well-established ways of work and life, it is not surprising that many of us are slow to learn. Better to try harder at familiar tasks, we think, than to face the possibility that experience may be calling us to move beyond them.

This is not to urge people to drop their jobs or to flee to new settings. For myriad reasons, neither course may be open to many people. Obligations and/or felt immobility keep some men and women from making any external changes. But *external* change is not the only possibility and is rarely the desirable first move. Changes may begin by first recognizing the instruction inherent in de-illusionment. The acknowledgement that something different is afoot is the first and necessary step. Such an acknowledgement involves the realization that nothing in our life is going to be quite the same as it has been. Although few things have remained unchanged over the decades, the emerging dislocations will not be akin to earlier tremors. What is in the process of happening is of an order of magnitude for which few are prepared. We are being given the opportunity to recognize the idolatries inherent in what we thought was the covenant-faithfulness of preceding decades of work and human involvements. In aging we are privileged to recognize as illusions what we had been led to believe were our deeply held convictions. Some illusory ingredients are in certain ways inseparable from our treasured convictions. In aging we have an opportunity to step outside the system by which we have been defined, to recognize, with candor but without bitterness, the provisional, sometimes even dishonest, character of its lures and rewards. For the first time since childhood our eyes are opened and we are free to acknowledge and to report what we see for the benefit of others.

Perhaps my perspective on these matters will be clearer if we recall Hans Christian Andersen's tale of "The Emperor's New Clothes." Embodying a highly romanticized view of childhood, the fable reminds us that despite pressure to conform there are always some people who refuse to go along with language that uses a term like "Peacemaker" to designate a nuclear weapon. Masses may assent to such wordplay; some are unable to do so. Like the child in Andersen's story who announces the king's nakedness, those who cannot go along with such societal disinformation are, in my judgment, its servants rather than its betrayers. And they are rarely children!

Because they are often free of illusions about both the value of social conventions and their own rectitude, the aged are ordinarily more clear-sighted than those still in the system are able to be. Some younger people may be among those who recognize the king's nakedness, yet many elders may continue to play the game of public illusions. (What we see or do not see is not in any absolute way a matter of age. I would not be guilty of transferring to the aged Andersen's romanticism about the children's discernment.) Their complicity is the consequence of attitudes toward aging that keep elders from the vocation of social criticism to which I believe God would call them. (Social criticism often erupts from the disadvantaged. Unfortunately, the criticism of inequality is often silenced by the creation of some measure of opportunity for those raising the protest.) My concern is to challenge a sizable group of people who can abandon some of the society's enchantments with a minimum of bitterness to provide an ongoing cadre of witnesses. Beyond illusions about the system and concerned for universal human well-being, they are people God can use.

Alternatively, by far the greater number will accommodate too comfortably both to society's definition of what it means to grow old and to the provisions made for aging so (mis-) understood. It is from the elderly who have been called by God that we should hear parade-route announcements about nakedness, homelessness, hunger, and the evil of the misuse of language. It is grandmother and grandfather, through their long experience and, more important, their gradual detachment from society, by whom we should be alerted to those perils which the majority of us usually prefer to ignore. That there are few such clarion voices indicates either how faulted is my thesis or how coopted are the aged by a society which really has no use for them. To put the latter more accurately: intuiting the disclosures of which the elderly are capable, society finds diversions, often pleasant for the privileged, which keep them quiet.

COUNTERCULTURE AS AN OPTION

Whatever our eventual assessment of the views of other societies toward aging, the immediate imperative is to realize why, in this society, a countercultural attitude is one of the few positive options for the aged. Among the alternatives are a pretence of youthfulness, resignation to the fact of failure, flight from the present into nostalgia, or illness. The latter is, in part, a matter of volition in an ageist society. To a degree at least, an inhospitable environment is sickening. One does not feel well in a setting that repeatedly fails to encourage the business one would pursue. Nobody finds trivialization enhancing.

A central feature of a viable—by which I mean healthy—society is the adequacy of its provision for the needs of a highly diverse citizenry. Among the varied elements of that diversity are people at the many stages of human life from cradle to grave. These stages bring developmental opportunities over the course of a life. For as long as one lives there is no way to avoid passing through adolescence, early adulthood, mid-life, and the various phases of growing older. In far greater detail than Shakespeare's Seven Ages, contemporary theorists of human development identify and describe multiple stages, each characterized by its distinctive tasks and by being part of the continuity of life. This conjoined emphasis is crucial to my argument that, although there are somewhat recognizable phases through which all who live must pass, *the humanly significant fact is the continuity of a life*. However important is each of life's stages in itself, all are finally justified by their contribution to the *whole* person's formation. In my understanding, *all* of life's stages are successively important to human maturation. That this is not a societal conviction is the source of what I believe to be aging's most serious and sweeping problem: *there is no adequate societal provision for the maturation latent in the later years*. Lacking such encouragement, or even permission, older people are often driven to one of the options mentioned above. The lure of wholeness, which I take to be from God and intrinsic to the work of the later years, is—given societal neglect—simply abandoned by many men and women. The cost of this involuntarily arrested development, that is, the need to pretend that there are no sequels to the growth inherent in mid-life, is paid for by the myriad individuals trapped in pretense and by the entire society. By truncating the stages in which development may occur we attempt to substitute a part of life for the whole story. Our ideological attitude toward life's productive decades as normative for all ages not only fails to encourage growth to life's end, but drives some to fashion a counterculture.

At least one additional clarification is required for my thesis: namely, that potential for human maturation persists to death. Although deathbed conversions are relatively rare, such a marked reversal—or even the appearance of it—demonstrates the vitality of a life even at death's door. Given the importance of the unending human potential for change, it is probably necessary to examine the persistent popular assumption that the completion of physical growth completes a person's maturation. Nothing could be more inaccurate nor, for my purposes, more unfortunate than this misunderstanding. It is true that by the time an individual is physically mature a good deal of the shape of his or her life is in place; at least *some* of the resources with which a person copes with further experience are at hand.

In the following decades of adulthood and aging, however, vastly more and markedly more complex events occur. While a person lives, there is no way to escape the varied experience of being a particular person living through unforeseeable personal and public events. Every day there are unanticipated familial and societal circumstances with which people cope. Over time these changing circumstances influence both a person's resources for coping and the person he or she is becoming. The mother of small children, for example, may become the grandmother of small children. Given the passage of time, however, she cannot be the same nurturing person in both relationships. Her later capacity for nurturance, which may well be greater, is unavoidably different because of her earlier experience and all else that has intervened. She may want different things for her grandchildren from those she sought for her own children. For as long as we live we may never fully escape the potential for being instructed by our experience. The possibility of further growth persists to life's end. *The potential for significant personal growth never ends.* Regrettably, most people decline the repeated opportunities for this continuing maturation. Whether we affirm or decline the opportunities remains to the end a matter of individual decision. God does not force us to choose the risky paths to greater life. Despite protestations to the contrary, our society discourages risk taking in the area of personal maturation. Furthermore, all people are not alike in their ability to make decisions. It is my hope that by helping society to encourage later life developments human inequalities that are not expungeable will be ameliorated.

Of equal importance, however, is my belief that God's graceful but resistible instruction may be seen in many of the attitudes so often changed by time's passage. This is to insist that in addition to the instruction inherent in major biological shifts, no less important tutelage may occur simply with the passage of time. The mode of pedagogy changes from biology's traumas to history's gradualism. The grandmother who has become a different nurturing person from the person she was as a young mother illustrates my contention as the physical change of menopause does not. The end of a woman's menstrual cycle may be the occasion of profound attitudinal changes because her sexual life no longer holds the potential for pregnancy. Love and the reproductive capacity have been instructively separated by biological changes.

Whereas earlier in life important instruction often arose from biological changes—puberty being the most dramatic of these developmental promptings—*these changes are less instructive in later life than is the passage of time.* This, which I see as evidence of God's effort to instruct us through ordinary experience in history rather than nature, is probably less coercively instructive than are the more obvious biological changes. Those who are determined to avoid change have varied means for ignoring encouragement, from whatever source, to modify their outlook. Neither these powers to resist what I identify as God's ordinary means of tutelage, nor the fact that aging's developmental promptings are separable from any biological changes, must obscure my contention that, with time's passage, attitudes change appropriately.

It is because of such convictions that I advance as a positive option for older people a countercultural stance. Not only are we as a society apparently careless about the potential for growth over the decades of adulthood—as though we did not notice those countless opportunities—we are largely blind to the agenda which gradually emerges as we grow old. It is so convenient to assume that after a particular birthday relatively early in adulthood, a person forever remains unchanged. That there is continuity to a life is an important belief: the truth teller and the liar probably remain in character over the decades. Depending on the experience to which they have been subject, however, and the encouragement to continued growth, few people will be at sixty what they were at thirty. Like flowers, lives will unfold. With time's passage one's perspectives on most things change. It is simply not possible at retirement to view the world and oneself as one did on entering the work force—or, often, even as one did a decade earlier. This is not to deny that some younger persons are able to empathize with the perspectives of their elders. The occasional ability to do this depends on an imaginative capacity arising from the ability to transcend their own outlook. A more likely factor in bridging perspectives is that older people, having lived through the earlier stages, can remember how they felt, yearning for things for which they have now lost at least some taste. Although hardly an easy assignment for all, or even possible for some, remembering may be the easier task than youth's imaginative anticipating. Even so, many older people utterly block such ability to empathize with those who are younger, and some youth have remarkable empathy with the aged.

People's varied recollective abilities, which help to maintain aging's continuity with those who are younger, do not constitute the entirety of what we are calling the emerging agenda of life's later years. These new "assignments" arise from perspectives which have gradually changed over the decades. At the point, for example, when one realizes that there is less time left than one has already lived, neither the world nor the self continues to appear as they once did. Sensibilities have undergone real but usually nontraumatic modification; tasks once imperious have given way to others once unimaginable. It may be that the ordinarily imperceptible, incremental change in outlook over the decades—so different, for example, from adolescence's often dramatic shifts—contributes to our inability to recognize aging's somewhat distinctive emerging agenda. Ordinarily these outlooks change *gradually*, which although developmentally fortunate, may also make them harder to notice and easier to ignore.

Whatever the causes of our blindness, the fact is that, as a society, we make almost wholly inadequate provision for aging's "course work." Not only do we not encourage that, we seem to have a positive distaste for it. Such repulsion arises, I suggest, from the fact that aging's business is in some important ways at sharp variance with the busyness of one's earlier years. To insist that if they want others to approve, the elderly must continue to behave as they once did, desire what they once wanted, enjoy what once gave pleasure, is—in many instances and in varying degrees—to require pretense. This is no less abhorrent in aged persons feigning youthfulness than in youth pretending a maturity that eludes them. *Always the challenging task is to be able to act one's age.* Never easily overcome, since there is always more to us than any present appearance can suggest, the difficulty is compounded when discouragement is encountered instead of societal encouragement. Given our idolatry of adulthood's outlook, I sense increasing resistance rather than encouragement to the tasks of both youth and age. We seemingly cannot sufficiently accelerate one group's passage *into* adulthood, and we cannot tolerate the suggestion that the other wants to get *out of* the familiar mainstream. Is it surprising that both the young and the old, who have *much* more in common than we ordinarily recognize, are inclined to be countercultural? *Adulthood's curse is its inability to honor attitudes and values other than its own.*

Yet not all stages of life are capable of adulthood's uncritical enthusiasm for production and consumption. Not all periods of life hold the same ultimate values. Society's inability to grasp this is what drives some youth and their elders in a countercultural direction. For their development they require attitudes quite different from the narrow commercial criteria. Attitudes and behaviors which those in the middle decades may see as sheer folly may be necessary urgencies for both youth and age. Attuned to the beat of different drummers, at odds with the dominant rhythm, they seek a more diverse and supportive culture than is ordinarily available for their distinctive tasks.

About youth's development others have written and will continue to write. Our immediate work is to begin to suggest why older people often find themselves at odds with prevailing values. We are concerned here with the ways in which older people's perspectives gradually change. Please note that I am not insisting on the applicability of these views to all other age groups. That is *not* my intent. However, just as it would be inappropriate to insist that all ages see the world as do the aged, so, in my judgment, is it wrong to require them to continue to espouse without change the outlooks of their earlier years. I want only for older people to be free to get about whatever may be their own agenda. That their break with the past is never total should not obscure the fact that important modifications are afoot. Over time modest degrees of change will result in a new outlook.

Especially since my understandings may be unfamiliar to some, it is imperative to emphasize the observation that underlies what I have to say about particular perspectival changes. *I contend that by the simple passage of time*, which happens inescapably while we live, *our outlooks change.* The very people who once could not imagine living in one room in a retirement center, without most of the possessions they earlier thought were necessary to their identity, may respond, "That was then. This is now." Those incapable of that profound grasp of the impact of time's passage—those whom experience fails to instruct, those holding tenaciously to attitudes and expectations once appropriate—are doomed to late-life unhappiness. They are pathetically unable to move beyond an outlook that held only temporary validity. We *cannot* remain forever young parents or novices at work. Accumulated experience, which the passage of time makes possible, carries us beyond our initial inexperience. Neither within our domestic life nor in the workplace is it possible to remain forever naive. Whatever else it may mean, déjà vu acknowledges that the unfamiliar does not remain that.

I contend further that such opportunities for instruction, although they are hardly as dramatic as puberty's biological upheavals, are comparable stimuli to growth. The fact that there need be no marked biological components, as in adolescence, should not blind us to the pedagogy inherent in experience itself. Time inescapably passes; outlooks may change. Clearly, there is no assurance that all people will be equally instructed by the experiences which ineluctably accumulate. But not even the traumatic changes of adolescence assuredly move all young people toward maturity. Many remain juveniles, some revert to the apparent safety of childhood despite the horrendous cost of backward movement; most, fortunately, are instructed by youthful experience and move forward. Just as their movement is never uniform nor uninterrupted, so it is with older people whom experience instructs. They know the need to vacate old territories and are attracted to incipient growth. At any stage of life, however, there is a price to pay for such development. What we may come to view as a fair charge, or even a bargain, should not obscure the fact that no maturation is ever cost-free.

The question that must not be obscured, but which society does not always encourage us to see, is this: might it be *costlier* to decline an opportunity for growth than to attempt the risk? Although people answer the question differently at all significant junctures for potential growth, and although there is no universally valid single timetable for such maturation, for the long range it is always preferable to have greater access to the fathomless depths of the self. In those depths lies the key both to one's kinship with humankind and to the knowledge of God. From such awarenesses on the edge of mystery emerge energies for the tasks at hand and appreciation for the ways in which all things are new. Déjà vu is not the last word for those who assent endlessly to the risks of growth. Novelty may erupt from the familiar.

About the particulars of aging's developmental opportunities, older people will not necessarily agree. No single explanation of aging satisfies everybody. Even the processes of *physical* aging are not explainable to the satisfaction of all. These things being the case, and given society's inhospitable attitudes toward aging, I have taken the liberty to identify some of the important areas in which outlooks change over time. Since these are changes *away from* prevailing attitudes and older people may feel an urgent desire to get on with their distinctive growth, I am proposing an understanding of aging as inescapably countercultural.

THE POSSIBILITIES FOR CHANGE

Changes in outlook, occurring involuntarily—things not willed but apparently inseparable from the passage of time— are part of God's continuing opportunities for instruction. Since some people will be unsympathetic with such a way of thinking, and others who consider themselves religious will find my approach unfamiliar, it might be helpful to indicate some of my most salient assumptions. First, as indicated in Chapter 2, "Experience and Faith," I affirm an ongoing dialectical relationship between these essential aspects of human life. Held together, experience and faith mutually inform, challenge, and deepen without ever controlling each other. To attach such importance to ordinary experience will be off-putting to those who believe that God is to be known only in special revelations. Such offense as may be taken is more than offset in my mind by the realization that my outlook has a long and honorable history. Two illustrations—one ancient and one contemporary—will suffice. In his *Confessions*, Augustine wrote as follows in the course of accounting for his conversion to and maturation in Christian faith: "In this way my personal experience enabled me to understand what I had read."[2] Rightly understood, experience and faith illumine each other. The current, consonant emphasis is in the published criteria for the selection of poetry for a Catholic monastic quarterly.

> We try to find poems that do not refer *directly*, self-consciously to God or to religious experience, but rather poems that evoke the depths of *human* experience which is always pregnant with God. Since God is not a separate being but Being itself, we look for poems that depict our response to Being, whom we meet in muck, manure, blood, sweat, wrestling, swimming, chasing dogs, mourning, dancing, etc. Thus, like the ancient Jews, we shy away from mentioning his name directly in poetry, for fear of separating it from the life that utters it.[3]

Given the nature of Being, experience will lure to more adequate faith-formulations only by indirection . Please note that despite my insistence on their inseparability, I am not equating experience with God's grace. What I contend is that the instruction latent in human experience in history, that is, in the passage of time, is God's ordinary means of tutelage. To the extent that people undertake the risks inherent in lifelong growth, they will unavoidably need to ground those lives at ever greater depths. Thus, God becomes ever more thoroughly and precisely the gracious God as we struggle again and again to act our age. Inherent in the struggle is the need for a willing faith in Being itself. Experience both instructs and drives us to ever-greater depths of instruction. All such tutelage is from God.

Despite my appreciation for their inherent complementarity, my second assumption is that faith and experience compete endlessly to exercise decisive influence in a life. Whatever the reasons, most of which have been labeled as sin, aptitudes that should be complementary try to dominate each other. The disorder inherent in experience threatens to eliminate the human penchant for order; and faith's impetus for systematization threatens to subdue all vestiges of chaos. The competition, which is at least as old as the tensions between the Apollonian and the Dionysian forces in ancient Greece, will not disappear. There will be times when society tips one way, then the other; something similar will obtain in seasons of individual lives. Rarely and briefly, but beautiful when it happens, faith and experience will take each other seriously. The later years could be such a time for many people. Some combination of disenchantment with societal rewards (How big a house is big enough? How long a vacation is long enough?), the growing awareness of life's brevity, and a paradoxical concern for the well-being of future generations, may be among the factors that enhance this possibility in aging.

Third, it is probably important to acknowledge that these changes that I associate with time's passage are (like all experiences) not *necessarily* instructive. However, since we seem as a society willfully determined to maintain the illusion that nothing necessarily changes with the passage of time—as though human will were an absolute capability—I find it imperative to insist that, whether acknowledged or not, *everything is influenced by time's passage*. Nothing remains unchanged over time. The problem is that, being unable to reconcile change with the desire to be in control in the old ways in an unchanged world, we try resolutely to ignore change's inevitability. The negative effects on a biblical spirituality of this determination to deny change are ominous. Not only are older people discouraged from getting on with their appropriate agenda, but they are encouraged, even required, to *pretend* nothing has changed. Apart from the special circumstances and purpose of the theater, pretense is never a basis for maturation. The sad fact is that the more one is inclined to pretense, the more assured it is that the reality of inevitable change will fail to instruct. This is to say that those who will be most incapacitated for aging's exciting work will be those who have bought most uncritically into the spirit of the times. Regrettably, that spirit exhorts us to shut our eyes to whatever today may seem to be different from yesterday. We are not the first society to believe in its ability to obscure the effects of time's passage.

From the perspective of those who endlessly need to feel that they are in control of their lives, yesterday, today, and tomorrow are said to be identical. This emotionally derived emphasis on continuity is obviously at odds with the strident voices of those who insist that today's products are significantly different from those that were huckstered yesterday. Could both of these apparently dissimilar emphases be wrong, as I believe? In my understanding it is equally false to deny the consequences of time's passage for changed perspectives as it is to engage in the vendor's sleight of hand. In only a very limited sense is a freshly painted product "brand new." Should I have said sleight of mouth? Although sales may decline should the market place follow my understanding, this clarification is basic: *continuity characterizes products, discontinuity marks lives.* The challenges that many people avoid in the area of personal growth they try to compensate for by enthusiasm for the lies about this year's novelties. Things acquired will not make up for growth declined. That is an iron law!

By contrast, the nurturing work of the Holy Spirit will enable us to embrace today's *un*familiarity on the assumption that no two days—or eras of a life—are ever identical for those who profess belief in the *living* God. Minimally, such faith need be no more instructive than this: it is God's will that

things change. Novelty, which is the invitation to move beyond
what we were yesterday, is the inescapable consequence—the
good gift—of the nature of the God who continues to make all
things new. That we abhor that novelty which challenges us,
while we are enamored with whatever is commercially novel,
only suggests why, for some aged persons, their only option is
to learn how to live against the grain. Inasmuch as their souls
are at stake, it is imperative that they not look in vain for
encouragement in such demanding work. I see in our society
no other sources of such support than the religious communities, especially those in the biblical tradition, which are committed to enhancing the wholeness of human lives made in the
image of God. Not only does such a belief undergird the
sacredness of the great variety of lives in all their stages, but
it continually urges men and women to move toward the
realization of their unique potential. That the goal may never
fully be realized in history in no way invalidates the faith-
informed risks of moving through life's stages. What I have
identified as a vocation for the later years both arises from
historical experience and transcends it. Thus is one's calling
one's true life: rooted in nature and history but confineable to
neither.

With these three self-disclosures in mind—my assumptions
about the inherent complementarity of faith and experience,
about their respective imperialisms, and about the understanding that nothing is universally and equally vividly instructive—we may begin to discuss four of the many *changes
which I believe may come about with the passage of time.* In the
order for discussion these are (1) a growing realization of the
myriad, powerful, prevailing, but misleading opinions about
aging, (2) the emerging awareness of how little of our lives is
actually ours, (3) the discovery that we have more in common
with others than we differ from them, and (4) the impetus to
simplify our lives. Those elderly who find themselves equipped
with such simple but potent alternatives to the prevailing
ideology will be the cadre of God's prophetic witnesses for
changes appropriate to the new century.

About these—and such other developments as often come

with time—at least two prefatory statements are needed. First, some people will deny having experienced any of these stirrings, and probably nobody will experience them all equally. Second, all such developments of later life are at odds with prevailing social values and attitudes. This suggests why taking a countercultural stance may be the unavoidable route for some seniors. On these assumptions we may identify some elements of the instruction that the passage of time makes possible. My understanding of such enlightenment as God's ordinary pedagogy may be unfamiliar to some.

First, as we grow older, many people gradually recognize the extent to which their minds have been riddled with inaccuracies about aging. Before identifying a few of these, it is important to emphasize the inadequacy of speaking of these views as mere errors. *Inaccurate* they are, but the word does not begin to suggest their prevalence and power. *These ideas are not simply mistakes; they are part of our ideology.* If mere errors, they would be as easy to correct as an arithmetic miscalculation. As ideology, they are mistakes we cannot revise without unsettling our lives. They function as do myths, enabling us to give order to otherwise conflicted realities. If some virtue may be recognized in a change often associated with growing old—greater willingness to acknowledge dependency—then our ideological emphasis on the necessity of independence will be somewhat unsettled. The sad fact is that as a people we are not equipped to affirm such ambivalences. Tensions between independence and dependence do not yield, as does simple error, to recalculation. In our antipathetic attitudes toward aging we touch an important nerve of our society that asserts that *it is imperative to avoid any positive understanding of what growing old might mean.* Our negative attitudes might well be identified as part of our theology, of which there are always both orthodox and heretical versions. From the perspective of public "theology," or myth, or inaccuracies about aging, my efforts to advance a positive view constitute the heresy.

Since identifying the ideological character of our attitudes is markedly the most important goal, some people may be helped to such recognition by naming a few of the rampant inaccuracies. How true, for example, are these popular assumptions about old people: that senility is inescapable? that memory loss is one obvious ingredient of senility and contributes to the inability to learn? that the loss of sexual interest and capability is but one of the consequences of a general loss of physical strength? As the assumed result of these inaccurate assumptions, many people believe that old people cannot grow. Drawing on a faulty analogy from horticulture, the attitude seems to be that, like a plant, humans proceed from seed to flower to fruit to ripe fruit to rot. A fine description of the tomato season, the analogy is utterly inappropriate for *human* life. Among other basic facts overlooked, human beings are never merely natural in this way. In my understanding a human life continues to ripen for as long as a person continues to risk ever more through self-acquaintance.

About the prior popular assumptions need we do more than two things? First, we can admit that, of course, all the symptoms mentioned are true for some. Senility and its consequences *do* happen. Second, we can ask what it is that requires society to treat that which is limitedly true as though it were universal? Here is the social pathology I most want to expose. That extrapolation is what prompts me to the conclusion that, for aging to be gracefully possible in our context, older people must learn a countercultural stance.

To the second awareness that time's passage makes possible we have already devoted an entire chapter: we hardly own the lives we have led (see Chapter 4). Encouraged to pursue an abundance of experience—the title of an insufficiently popular film about tourism in Europe comes to mind, *If It's Tuesday, It Must Be Belgium*—our lives have been characterized by rush rather than by reflection. The underlying assumption is classic: in order to live meaningfully one must simply accumulate ever more and more varied experience. Quantity is the key to significance. Neither too large a house nor too long a vacation is possible. Big is always beautiful.

With the passage of time one of two reactions is possible to the quantitative formula. Some people in the later years either try to accumulate additional experience in ever more desperate efforts to add meaning to their lives, or they begin to wonder about the validity of the assumption. For the former I find nothing but compassion; in the latter I sense hope. For some of those who become uncertain about the adequacy of busyness to sustain an aging life, the diminution of energy is itself the first of God's enlightening gifts. What keeps us from recognizing fatigue as a means of grace? How better to learn about the futility of an undertaking than to discover our lack of energy for it? Although there is occasionally a medical cause of such diminishment, the far more frequent explanation lies elsewhere. It is quite appropriate to wonder about the means God may employ in redirecting the focus of one's life. Does God energize only the believer? From rush to reflection is an inherently spiritual change which, in many instances, may be aided by the onset of fatigue.

Whereas rush is an effort to hold everything, including personal experience, at arm's length, reflection presupposes the willingness to sift through experiences and to encounter the self's varied reactions, over time, to their multiplicity. Self-avoidance or self-acquaintance, but not both, will be the progressive option in aging. It is not, I believe, inaccurate to recognize the former as self-abandonment, possibly becoming resignation to a life irretrievably lost. By contrast, to undertake the risks of self-acquaintance is to put oneself in the way of possibly coming to know God in the process of reclaiming one's always ambivalent life. Such knowledge is not assuredly forthcoming even when the risk is ventured. Unlike the deadening route of self-avoidance, however, such efforts at self-reclamation assure the *possibility* of finding oneself in God's presence.

A society that urges maximization of experience while minimizing reflection at first stimulates and then bores. The combination precludes the possibility of that integration which is a distinctive human achievement. Since the desire for a more humane life often accompanies aging, is it surprising that older people may become countercultural in an environment that undervalues reflection's integrative work? Only the realization that their souls are at issue will encourage some to risk the disapproval to which all deviancy is subject. The dominant ideology will have a disapproving word. Fortunately, it is not the last word. That Word is that we are inseparable from the lives we have led (God-as-truth-evoker) and that by God's grace we may own the lives we have lived. Such resources as we have, and they are always limited, are the inescapable consequence of our prior choices. This is the iron law: that nothing is added to whatever we have acquired. What we lack we cannot give. However, the potential for doing some good inheres in what we have and are. The consequence of God's grace is that by reflection we begin to see the limited good of which we are capable. Thus, the iron law endures but no longer imprisons.

The third discovery that often arises from the passage of time may be the most surprising of those we are discussing. It may also be the most unburdening. Having for decades been encouraged to establish a distinctive identity, and having eagerly and repeatedly undertaken the work, it gradually dawns on some people *how much more like others* they are than unlike.

This is not to suggest, after the manner of the Upanishads in particular and Hinduism in general, that, like a drop of water momentarily blown free of the ocean, our sense of individual life is an illusion. I am committed to the assumption that there is something inherently indissoluble, something enduringly distinctive, about personal life. Identity may be flawed without being an illusion.

In our setting, however, individualism is unwarrantedly inflated. So overblown is this emphasis that it burdens and blinds us. We are required to feign an utter distinctiveness which the facts belie. Possibly excepting the phenomenon of identical twins, we are not physically equatable with anybody else. Given our varied experience—even siblings are not born into quite the same family—no two people will see anything in exactly the same way. Such are family dynamics that our perspective depends in part on our place in the order of births. In my judgment, however, it is not possible to fashion a persuasive rationale for a radical individualism on these flimsy bases.

That we are never collapsible into a herd identity, are always something more than a member of a group, means that there is an enduring distinctiveness to each life. Without insisting on the absoluteness of individual life we may also affirm its reality.

At least of equal importance, however, is our similarity to others. Without attempting here to document the overwhelming evidence of the social character of our lives, let me simply label as hopelessly burdensome the obligation to present oneself so as to conceal the myriad evidences of our likeness to all other persons. It is as important to recognize our kinship with others as it is to emphasize our difference from them. Again, time's passage may instruct us about this dialectic. Is it any less miraculous to be unburdened from the obligations of an extreme individualism by being able to recognize our kinship than were Jesus' gifts of sight to the blind? Is the physical inability to see significantly more restrictive than the blindness inherent in an individualistic ideology which that requires us to deny burdensome facts about our likeness to others?

Similarities which, in earlier years, we simply could not see—or could not afford to see (does it really matter which it is?)—often become gradually recognizable and, moreover, seen as the God-given means by which to abandon inappropriate burdens long carried. Thus, as many people grow older, truth becomes more appealing than the ideology into which they were inducted. It is not, we may discover, a matter of maintaining individualism at all costs. The pretense we have maintained for decades may in time be recognizable for the very partial truth it has always been. If time's passage has given us the ability to see the falsity of the obligation to be utterly different, we may free ourselves of the weighty burden inherent in such attempted deception. Freed from this inappropriate obligation, the less self-deceived self is now able to take on burdens appropriate to a more accurate appreciation of oneself and kindred. By a surprisingly natural process, which is evidence of God's presence in our midst, we have been led from an ideologically induced, tedious isolation to a liberating aware-

ness of kinship. How much more dramatic must experience be
to qualify as rebirth? In the episode reported at length in the
ninth chapter of John's Gospel the young man whose life was
changed is able, when interrogated, only to repeat: "One thing
I do know, that though I was blind, now I see" (see John 9:15,
25, and 30).

Regrettably, those whom experience has instructed to move
beyond an ideological individualism will be no more welcome
than was the young man whom Jesus healed. Being able to
affirm *both* one's distinctiveness and one's likeness to others
will not sit well in a society determined to keep such realities
separated. As we have already said, the ideology will have a
disapproving word for those who deviate from its tutelage.
Fortunately, that is not the last word. That Word is, as in Jesus'
summary of Jewish law, that, in tandem with love for God and
of comparable importance, we are free to love both our neighbor (our kindred) and ourselves. In ways never to be fully
understood, though always relished, our true identity is inex-
tricable from these enduring relationships.

What alternative is there for those so instructed by time's
passage than to learn to withstand a culture unable to affirm
equally the self *and* the other?

The fourth of the eye-opening experiences that may accompany the passage of time has to do with a growing conflict
between the desire for simplification and the lure of possessions. Although the pattern was established long before Thorstein Veblen coined the expression, another aspect of the prevailing ideology is that we are an "acquisitive society."[4] We
have been told in a great variety of ways, which few are able to
ignore, that the more one has of this world's goods the better
person one is. That the formula is clearly fraudulent keeps few
from long and hot pursuit of a great variety of things. So
important is it to acquire that Ralph Waldo Emerson has
insisted that "Things are in the saddle/And ride mankind"
("Ode to W. H. Channing"). Such preoccupation with items to
be bought, which has hardly been diminished by the effects of
marketing techniques developed in the past half century, constitutes *the* American passion. Given our emphasis on con-

sumer goods and the growing numbers of our most competent young people today enlisted in work to enhance sales, is it inaccurate to see in these values and behaviors our society's true religion? That to which people give themselves whole-heartedly and uncritically *is* their faith. The ardor once associated with religious vocation may now be the key to a Madison Avenue position.

That some people are weaned away from this true "church" could be the most compelling evidence supporting my contention that time's passage may instruct. Having given themselves for decades to accumulating, which is the sacred work of true believers, it is amazing that some men and women become disenchanted with the supposed benefits of the "religious duties" of consumerism. They find themselves pondering their many possessions—what to do with them, where to store them. (The paradox of the garage sale has long intrigued me as an analogy to the first law of thermodynamics: nothing is ever lost. In such sales, unlike the potlatch in which wealth *destroyed* was believed to demonstrate wealth, goods merely exchange hands at prices dramatically lower than their original purchase cost. Though unheralded, such exchanges are true acts of devotion to the system: items that supposedly enhance a person's worth become the possessions of those who, unable to buy in at top dollar, gain access thus to virtue.)

A person's first garage sale, the public act to which believers are driven by inadequate space for storage, may be a first step toward life simplification. If so, it is important to recognize that the hand of God, if we may speak thus, worked this time in part through crowded closets, attics, basements, or garages. Belonging to the acquisitive society involves us, inescapably, in errors, the consequences of which we cannot forever escape. We buy things that we never really wanted or that, even more predictably, go out of style. In either case we lack heart for them. *To lack heart for something is not necessarily instructive; to have to move or otherwise make repeated provision for things that no longer interest us is often quite eye-opening.* Again, although most people stay with the system—the commercial, convenient neighborhood rental locker is an annex calculated to serve devotional need in an era of diminished domestic storage space—some are driven to desperate lengths by the desire to unload. Their faith has been deeply undermined. If not revived by some "preaching mission" or other—the February Presidential Birthday Sales come readily to mind—such people are in danger of becoming countercultural.

The point not to be lost is this: it is by instruction often inherent in time's passage, rather than by seductive voices from an alien world, that such people lose the faith. Something about the pedagogy inherent in growing older opens their eyes to the disinformation and false lures of a culture that values the possession of things above all else. Their efforts at simplification are neither ends in themselves, nor will they succeed if divestiture alone is their purpose. The point of time's possible instruction is that there is something more to being human than acts of acquisition. What that something more, or other, might be is sometimes cryptically referred to as love and always has to do with the well being of future generations. The pursuit of this goal can become the agenda of older people.

Yet again, the ideology will have a disapproving word for those who deviate from its tutelage. Fortunately, that is not the last word. That Word is about loving and using: whereas the ideology teaches us to love things and use people, people in later years may come upon contrary instructions about loving people and using things. The difference between those two understandings, although slight in wording, is crucial in importance.

THE UNIQUE POTENTIAL OF THE AGING

Every social system derives its energy and its elan from those varied aspects of the human potential which they emphasize or neglect. That American society has been exceptionally dynamic I would not for a moment deny. Among other negative evidences of this are the innumerable casualties along the road to success.

Although we began as a revolutionary movement, there seems to be little evidence of comparably radical criticism of prevailing arrangements. Outsiders will complain, of course, until they are either admitted to the system's privileges or destroyed. The learning inherent in time's passage can become the genesis of a vocation for the one social group that is both in and out of the system. Their voices are largely muted at present, yet my hope for society's reformed future lies with those older people who have learned from their long experience and continue to care about the future well-being of today's men and women. Not all older people will enlist in such a radical undertaking. Those who do so will discover a true vocation for their later years.

Recognizing the possibility that I am seriously in error about such evidences and/or pathologically paranoid, it still seems important to try to discover the reasons for the muting of the elderly and to recognize the means by which their silence is largely assured. The reasons lie initially in the largely dissimilar perspective of those within and those outside the system. We have long known that perceptions of reality vary with factors such as the time, place, circumstance, or gender of the perceivers. I intend no diminishment of these radical and awkward differences. What needs to be emphasized, however, in light of my basic distinction, is that these ordinary differences are between people who have in common their participation *in the system.* Their task is to accommodate disagreements within a society in whose durability all have a high stake. This is simply less true of the aged who grasp their God-given vocation. I must be careful not to overstate the difference between those on the inside and those aged without. Unlike the disadvantaged, whose criticism arises from their being excluded from the system—at least from its privileges—the elderly can never be wholly outsiders. At the very least they remember their decades of involvement. While their relishing of achievements may be somewhat and appropriately diminished, they have not utterly forgotten the pleasure of self-investment in important tasks or the satisfaction inherent in prevailing—or at least enduring. For these reasons they have a loving attachment to the system that challenged and rewarded them. Furthermore, because they are looking to the future, they are unable to think of destroying the system. To my way of thinking, this is the raw material of responsible criticism.

Partly because the elderly also recall their failures and disappointments, to say nothing of their concern for future generations with whom they feel kinship, they are aware of some of society's deficiencies. Especially because of their generativity (Erik Erikson's term for those whose identity is inseparable from the prospects of well-being for today's children and youth) they are given tongues with which to call attention to the emperor's state of undress—or overdress. Those elderly who are voiceless are not so just because of fatigue, which is among the myths that society spawns about aging, but because they either have no concern for the future or are more comfortable being seen but not heard. In fact, many may be happy to be out of *both* sight and hearing.

The aging have a distinctive qualification for taking up the vocation of social criticism. Unlike the disadvantaged who may be stilled by inclusion in the system, the elderly can criticize with an awareness of both the achievements and the awesome failures of the period of history through which they have lived. Rather than contributing the transient criticism of the disadvantaged, the elderly will be a more stable and enduring group of potential critics once their eyes have been opened to what may be God's calling to them in their latter decades. Rather than criticizing as a result of envy, the elder-as-social-critic will witness to the social gains and losses of the era of his or her life. Thus, although the energy of their witness will derive from personal experience the object of that witness will be what has happened to *lives in society* as they have observed it. In this activity for the sake of future generations, people will find seeds of that wholeness which has long eluded them. Without abandoning the importance of their individual lives the focus will be on desirable social changes. The elder critic of society will have moved beyond the wrong-headed narcissism of a merely individual or privatized understanding of human lives. Affirming both the determinative social context and the endless potential for individual initiative, they will both experience and be exemplars of a growing God-given wholeness which is perhaps not achievable until the later years of life.

The key to this emphasis is that the elderly, at least to a degree unlike their juniors, are *in* but, increasingly, not *of* the world. Although it would be personally more satisfying, because more clear cut, to insist on the absolute difference between those within and those outside the prevailing system, that distinction is not possible. Such a complete disjunction is precluded by the actual memories of those now outside and the eventual possibility that those presently engaged in the system will step out of it. Retirement is not necessarily the step to this awareness. Many who discover their later life vocations will indeed have their eyes opened by moving out of the system at or, more likely, after retirement. There is something significantly instructive in no longer having a recognizable role. Many others, however, will not be instructed by retirement. Committed to the continuing necessity of remunerative work, they will resist every threat to their continuing employability. Unable to imagine an existence without work, they may remain within the system until they die. We will look in vain for candidates for aging's vocation among those many who are so dependent.

The point about some of those who eventually discover their prophetic vocation is that well before they were either elderly or retired, they realize, sometimes without despair, the illusions that undergirded their participation in the system. They are among those who recognize that nothing is as fault-free as they had been led earlier to believe. Such loss of illusion is sometimes traumatic, yet it may also be but a healthy prelude to the vocation I urge for the aging. There is the potential for eventual recruitment to that countercultural vocation among some people, but it is not assured. That many will prefer almost any alternative suggests the power of the culture we must learn to resist.

Chapter 6

Aging As God's Design

At least two of the exhortations often heard in churches may be based on a premise of questionable accuracy. Both assume that change is subject to one's power of will. Believers are urged to become utterly new people and also to give up their lives. That these themes are somewhat distinctive to separate seasons of the Christian year only partly relieves the seeming contradiction. If but one is mistaken, at least 50 percent of the unwarranted burden laid on believers can be eliminated. If neither is true, as I suspect, men and women may be freed to respond to the real challenge to Christian practice: learning to claim their actual lives as God's gift. Our failure as Christians may be both in confusing this work with an unacceptable selfishness and in underrating its difficulty.

The first of these exhortations is heard most commonly in the season after Pentecost. Because something dramatic apparently happened to the disciples, as reported in Acts 2, it is often suggested that by the Holy Spirit's presence we are to become utterly new men and women. That no such radical and enduring change occurred in the disciples' lives is rarely acknowledged, but that is not allowed to modify the absoluteness of many a Whitsunday exhortation. Because little content is ever given to the ordinarily vague exhortation to radically new spirituality, churchgoers may feel momentarily that they have been challenged when they have only been misled. However much we may be encouraged to let it happen, God does not, even at Pentecost, give out new personalities. A new *attitude* toward our old being is a gift worth considering and celebrating, as we do in this book. Those who believe, or would like to, that change is comparatively easy to achieve will be uncomfortable with this "determinism." With Jesus (see Matthew 6:27), I hold that much about our lives is given and unchangeable. The only thing that matters—and we have a degree of control here—is our attitude toward whatever cannot be changed. Such a change, which itself may not lie fully within our power, is what enables us to see as God's blessing that which had been sometimes viewed as curse. Are we prepared to consider aging as another of God's ordinary blessings? If not, why not?

The other exhortation, heard at least throughout Lent, is to give up our lives. How many sermons have been based on the admonition to true followers of Jesus to deny themselves and take up their crosses? (See Matthew 10:38 or Mark 8:35.) Although there is no warrant in the text, certainly, for self-indulgence, neither that nor self-denial seems to me a helpful first step for those who may be trying to take Lent seriously. The relationship to the self is more subtle, more dialectical, than either indulgence or neglect recognizes. Something must be affirmed before it can be sacrificed; there is neither merit nor achievement in abandoning what we never had or never valued. So often ignored in much Christian exhortation, is it not first necessary to claim something before it can be renounced? It is that simple: we cannot give or give up what we do not have.

CHOICE AS THE BASIS OF SPIRITUALITY

Even though an explicit exhortation to self-denial may be lacking, it is often implied by a writer's emphases. The following comment in a British newspaper exemplifies the form this emphasis commonly takes: "the real essence of Christianity . . . would be better put as loving God and our neighbor, unconditionally."[1] In this instance, which is representative of most thinking in the church, a clergyman was responding to Margaret Thatcher's equally incomplete basis for morality: "As I understand it, the right to choose is the essence of

Christianity." This exchange illustrates the difficulty that even intelligent and well-meaning people have with valuing equally the three components of Christian life—God, neighbor, and self. Mrs. Thatcher's understanding of the value of choice to the self is as incomplete and therefore inadequate as is that of the cleric's reminder to love God and the neighbor. It is never appropriate to break off any of the components of the triad about which choices must endlessly be made. These ingredients, God, self, and neighbor, must be equally honored, though there is no formula to guide the decision maker with certainty. Where real choice is involved, nobody can avoid either the excitement or the apprehension. This combination is the price we pay—or is it the reward?—for being made for wholeness rather than fragmentation, for integrity rather than alienation. Regrettably, many decline their vocation to embrace both stimulation and fear in favor of one or the other—or neither. Passivity is the means by which both forms of arousal are avoided.

The ordinary way of avoiding such fearful stimulation is by routinely assigning greater value to one or two of the parts of the triad: the clergyman counterbalanced Mrs. Thatcher's overemphasis on the individual by a comparable overemphasis on God and neighbor. Because incomplete, both positions are inadequate; and the clergyman's emphasis, if unmodified, denies access to the only thing one may know with any certainty, namely, one's own experience. Although such experience is *not* all that matters, there is no hope for responsible decision making until one begins to acknowledge what one's experience has been. As we have seen in discussing the relationship of faith and experience, the inescapability of choice is a distinguishing mark of modernity. *Only as we begin to claim our actual lives do we have the basis for a mature spirituality.* Such maturity does not stop with attention to the self; in pursuit of a genuinely human life, self-understanding takes full account of our relationship to both God and neighbor. For maturity to be possible, however, we must begin with what we can know.

There is no assurance that such self-knowledge will lead to maturity. However, in trying to claim one's life, there is the possibility one will recognize both one's kinship with all other men and women and be carried into a relationship with God, rather than fall victim to the despair which always lingers around self-acquaintance. Neither of the alternative emphases—focusing on God or neighbor to the exclusion of self as the route to reality—avoids the risk of abandoning the self entirely. Both of these emphases have been stressed over the centuries, often to the exclusion of attention to oneself. Thus, especially to the unthinking, such language is "religious," in contrast to my emphasis which is labeled "secular" at best. Such an understanding has always been misleading and has become especially inadequate in the late twentieth century. In the interest of whatever may be God's purposes in the emerging religious pluralism, such misunderstandings of the focus of religion must be resisted. Although the realm of selfhood is endlessly complex and often frustrating; and although the self is always tempted to claim unwarranted finality for itself, and although, as presently understood, it yields a distorted sense of all that is external to the self, *it is where we are at the moment.* However slippery the footing, I see nowhere else to start the search for a mature humanity that will encompass in dynamic and rarely stable balance the demands and needs of neighbor, self, *and* God. Such maturity can be distinguished by its refusal to make decisions on the assumption that one or two of the triadic ingredients are by definition *always* more important than the third. Willingness to honor all three is a rare and beautiful achievement.

It is important to avoid seeming to claim too much too easily about access to this present self. As all those know who write about autobiography, accurate self-presentation is a rarity. Nowadays it is a common opinion of students of autobiography that a direct approach to the self is the least likely way of disclosing the self. The desire for presenting oneself in the most favorable light is apparently inextinguishable.

Fortunately, there are alternatives to such directness. None is more promising than the last part of Jesus' summary of Jewish Law: "And . . . you shall love your neighbor as yourself" (Matthew 22:39). This double, interrelated exhortation to love reveals the means by which we may get acquainted with our present self: by paying attention to events that impinge on the life of our neighbor as on our own. These events will range from such massive social dislocations as war and financial catastrophe to changes in individual fortunes for good or ill. In loving our neighbor, we may identify with the neighbor who suffers or rejoices. In our reaction to what happens to the neighbor, we gain insight into ourselves. It is through this somewhat indirect means of recalling our reactions to some of the myriad events over a lifetime that we get some glimpses into the person we have become. It is not always a lovely discovery, to be sure, but it is made possible by forgiveness. What we are able to see about ourselves is inseparable from the extent of our awareness of God's grace.

Let us consider again the two themes often heard in churches: the implication for a new being for believers through the advent of the Holy Spirit, and the Lenten emphasis on losing, or abandoning, one's life. Lively alternatives to these misleading exhortations are to be found in the texts appropriate to Pentecost and Holy Week.

In the sermon reported in Acts 2, in which he undertook to interpret the unfamiliar event of people speaking in tongues, Peter quoted a familiar passage from the Hebrew Bible. As part of his effort to ground the day's ecstatic happenings in the recognizable Jewish past, to demonstrate the *continuity* of these events with earlier expectations about the advent of God's Spirit, Peter cited the prophesy from Joel 2:28:

> In the last days it will be, God declares,
> that I will pour out my Spirit upon all flesh,
>
> . . . .
>
> and your young men shall see visions,
> and your old men shall dream dreams.

(Acts 2:17)

What he said also suggests that the new life which is the Holy Spirit's gift to us *must* begin with the ability to claim our lives as they have been and now are. There is no new ground to occupy instantly. We did not become what we are overnight,

and such change as the Spirit may urge in us will be comparably gradual. (This may be an especially repugnant view to a
society which has been seriously misled about instantaneity:
what may be possible by adding hot water to various products
is utterly inapplicable to the slow and painful work of change
in any human life. Even the training of animals requires
patience increasingly rare among those accustomed to instant
gratification.) The disciples did not become new men overnight.
(See, for example, Peter's vacillation about conditions for
church membership in Acts 15 and Paul's response in Gala-
tians 2.) As did the disciples, so shall we struggle to the end of
our lives to reembrace the visions appropriate to our youth and
to recognize the dreams of our old age through which we might
draw together the various disparate strands which have been
our life. As we grow older, these strands can be woven into a
more complete fabric. As we once saw visions that distinguished us from others, the effect of which was both invigorat-
ing and isolating, so now we dream dreams in which we are
energized by seeing how much like others we are. Isolation
gives way to the weaving of the more integrated thread of our
life into the larger human fabric to which we belong. Within
the continuity of life from cradle to grave, we must add the
wholeness that dreams make possible to the individuality of
youthful idealism.

Dreams and visions are meaningful gifts of the Spirit, necessary to our humanity and appropriate to the stages of life
through which, in the providence of God, we all pass. It is not
visions that the aged need. Such Spirit-gifts to those who are
old would be as inappropriate as gifts of stones in response to
the child's request for bread (see Matthew 7:9). Nor would
dreams be appropriate Spirit-gifts for the young. The work of
integration is not imperative then; sufficient experience has
not accumulated by that point in a life. *Both youth and age
share the task to embrace gladly the present as from God.* But
they contend with different dimensions of present time. Youth
needs promising visions about the future's possibility. Age, for
whom there is relatively less future than there once was, needs
dreams by which to weave together a meaningful story out of

the many ingredients that have made up a life. To deprive youth of its vision of a viable future, or to withhold from the old those dreams in which a meaningful past may be discerned, is to deny the possibility of gladly affirming the present as God's good gift. So much of life has this character—youth without hope, the aged with but isolated and isolating memories—that it is tempting to think that everything must be transformed for anything to deserve our attention. In an age of extreme emptiness, such as many find the present to be, the temptation is to overstate the possible sources of meaning in available experience. With the hyperbole of advertising already *the* vogue, the temptation is to overstate the gospel's reassurances. Although this may be appealing, it lacks scriptural warrant and is uncertain of fulfillment. Relying on overstated reassurance is poor preparation for those who must discover that life-in-the-spirit is a slow process that requires a lifetime for maturation. At the end time, says the prophet, the Spirit will see to it that all people—young, old, and all in between—receive those gifts which will enable them to assent to the living present.

As Peter's credibility on the first Pentecost depended on his ability to relate the unfamiliar happenings to what people knew, so the Spirit's presence in our lives cannot violate the need for continuity. There may be many things about present life that need to be changed. Such renewal depends on the initial ability to claim one's life as one's own rather than the ability to distance oneself from that life. Actually, the process of reclamation is endlessly repeated as more truth surfaces. That is the hard-because-unfamiliar truth we pursue here: the Spirit's first gift in the interest of an eventually changed life is the ability to see things about ourselves as they really are. The *paradox* of this gift of the Spirit is that if there is to be any eventual freedom, any emerging ability for love's sake to move beyond our present character, we must claim/affirm what has been true of our lives to date. As strange as the sequence may seem, we must acknowledge our bondage in the interest of possible eventual liberation.

Some may object that I have excised all of the mystery from

a central Christian event and promise. I can reply only that mystery remains central to my understanding of the Spirit's presence and work. What has been removed, or at least diminished, is the mystification by which some are temporarily fascinated and which many mistakenly believe central to Christianity. Rejecting both of these fallacies, I find it strangely exciting that the Spirit's initial work is to enable me to see myself more clearly, *as I would prefer not to do*. I then become able to lay claim to my actual life and begin to give God thanks for it. Such changes are inherently mysterious without being mystifying, challenging without trivializing.

There is no assurance that anybody will prefer the challenge of self-acquaintance to the mystifying claim that God does it all. The overwhelming evidence, including that about the disciples in the Gospels, is that people decline responsibility whenever possible. We prefer any alternative to the need to get acquainted with ourselves. But we may find the blessing of God's presence in the very wholeness from which we flee.

As is the case with Pentecost, so the corrective to the commonplace Lenten exhortation lies within the texts for Holy Week. In contrast to the glib encouragement to lose one's life, to deny oneself, we have detailed reports of Jesus in Gethsemane. Here we are given no superficial story of a man eager to abandon his life for God's sake, as though self-abandonment were an everyday matter. Exactly the opposite was happening. Although he recognized that events might have unfolded to the point of no return, Jesus clearly still valued his present life highly. Through his words we recognize and rejoice in his kinship with us: "If it be possible, let this cup pass from me" (Matthew 26:39). (That is, as we have often wished, I would be pleased if things could turn out differently from what I fear may be the unavoidable outcome.) These are the words of a man unmistakably like ourselves, a person loath to abandon the only life he assuredly knew. They are words that should be read in response to every glib exhortation to give up one's life.

It is because of these words that we have reason to take equally seriously those with which Jesus concludes his prayer: ". . . yet not what I want but what you want" (Matthew 26:39).

Having established his glad connection with his life as God's gift, Jesus' ability to relinquish it is among the reasons why we may believe that this man was the Messiah. Through these extraordinary words of submission which transcend ordinary experience we have the suggestion that God came as close to human life as God chooses to come. In this Jesus many have seen the God/man, valuing present life for the precious gift it is but declining to absolutize it. In this Jesus we have the model for claiming our actual life so that, at an appropriate time and as called upon to do so, we may give it up. The point of claiming one's life is neither to absolutize its importance nor to hide oneself away in its privacy. We exist both for the sake of the world and for our own sake. It is when both others and self are affirmed that we live to the glory of God. The glorious paradox is that it is only as we acknowledge our rootage in this world, only as we claim our actual lives, that we will be capable of being the blessing which lies deep within each of us to be. It is the glory of recognizing God's blessing in our ordinariness which, for love of neighbor and self, we struggle to recover. Lasting change, which is much rarer than popular culture would have us believe, is always a *gradual* process of letting go and taking on; if anything is to be abandoned it must first be lovingly possessed.

It is my hope, in what follows, to speak of the claims of Christian life in fresh ways while affirming a traditional gospel. I yearn to put the Christian claims in sufficiently different language that people may choose to affirm or decline them for what they really are, rather than for the misleading assurances often presented. I acknowledge that a presumption underlies the desire to put things so that nonbelievers might make an informed choice for or against Christianity. In the rapidly emerging pluralism of our time, many people will be loosened from their original religious moorings. In a bewildering era of a cafeteria of world religions, it is imperative that the appeal or repugnance of Christianity arise from accurate presentation of the gospel's claims.

CLAIMING THE PRESENT THROUGH FORGIVENESS

In the previous section we indicated how distorted religious exhortations undermine the work of reclamation. Such appeals are based on the assumption that *the* goal of religion lies *beyond* the present world. On this understanding the point is to get free from past and present life for the sake of an utterly different future. Many people believe this. What they fail to see is that any significant change in present and future life requires one to come to terms with—to reclaim—one's past life. There is no way short of insanity by which the past can be unhitched from either present or future. However much we may at times wish it otherwise, a human life is composed of these inseparable components: memory, anticipation, and the living present. It may never be easy to maintain a proper balance; an excess of either anticipation or reverie will undermine the liveliness of the present, to say nothing of their imbalancing effect on each other. And, since it is only now, at this moment, that God can be a living God for us, it is always the present which is at risk. However different the future may be from the present it will have to remain believably connected with one's earlier life. For one's later chapters to be related in this way to the earlier does not mean that they were foreordained. It does, however, mean that flowering has meaningful connections with earlier seeding and rootage. Poppy seeds do not produce peonies. Although not all seeds actually take root, the flowers of those that do could not have been other than they are. We are, I suspect, more like the plants than we ordinarily admit.

Whether or not there is any life beyond the present is a matter about which there is no verifiable knowledge. Those who choose to believe that there is such life stand on as sound (or unsound) ground as do those who remain agnostic. What is clearer to me than the unknowables of any future life is that, to be meaningful, any such life will have to be related to one's present life. For identity to persist there is no way that the future can be wholly detached from past or present. The work of reclamation is intrinsic to *human* life, which is distinguished by participating always in time past, future, and present. There is no way whereby one or other of these dimensions can be eliminated from human experience, though we often try to substitute a part for the whole and frequently emphasize one or the other.

As Christians, we are challenged to live in the present. The good news is that the gospel frees men and women to live in the present rather than to have to escape into either past or future. Youth are most apt to flee the intolerable present in favor of a vision-filled future, and the aging most often escape present guises by retreating into a nostalgia-filled past. But the Christian's work is, acknowledging both past realities and hopes for the future, to be present in the fullness of life at the God-given present moment. This sounds banal and unexciting only as long as we remain ignorant of how little of our immediate life is attuned to the present moment. Most of the time we are attentive to anything other than this moment, engaging in some reality-avoiding recollection or anticipation of something later in the day. In the present we must draw upon just whatever resources we possess. Gone is the pretense or the self-deception which are possible in (faulty) memory and (fanciful) hope. In neither past nor future am I limited to whatever I am and possess; in neither are there others who help to keep me honest about myself. Is it surprising that we often prefer *anything* to the present?

But the cards have been issued: there will be no new deal. Although imagination is an important "given" for present life, it cannot give us new resources. Nor is there any era other than our time in which we may live. Time, place, and capabilities for present life are not subject to change. So, is everything determined? Are we just to plod on until we die? Is that what it means that the cards are dealt? Is resignation the only alternative virtue?

Resignation is an important quality, but always in tandem with impatience. Not everything is unchangeable, and the most promising potential for significant change is in our attitude toward the hands we have been dealt. They were never intended to make us capable of anything and everything. They are capable of allowing *some* good work if we are able to assent to limited achievements.

Religious inhibitions to the work of self-reclamation do not

adequately explain why so much of so many lives is largely
unclaimed. In addition to the attempt to focus Christian attention on some possible future life, a second reason for this
neglect lies in popular attitudes toward the stages through
which all lives pass between birth and death. At times it seems
as though ignorance alone accounts for the widespread oblivion to these stages. That is surely part of the explanation. In
less sanguine moments, which are more frequent nowadays, I
sense that only willful indifference can account for the widespread failure to come to grips with one's past. The task is
being consciously avoided! Two suggestions come to mind in
this regard. First, it is in the tasks of life's successive stages
that the mobile ingredients of one's potential wholeness are to
be seen. Human life is endlessly unfolding, rather than ever
set at any age. Such dynamism means that the varied parts of
lives endlessly influence each other for change rather than for
stasis. At no time from birth to death is a human person ever
complete. Second, the potential for *different kinds of growth*
continues for as long as there is life. Old age may not permit
anything like the physical maturation of adolescence, or even
the intellectual growth of adulthood. Its spirituality is
grounded in memories recalled with feeling and hopes nurtured with care.

So understood, life's stages are at least as frightening to
some people as they are challenging to others. All people are
occasionally put off by the need for change; however, the
majority never see the challenges latent in their lives. They
prefer to pretend about the past rather than to seek an ever
larger and more accurate truthfulness about its actualities.
Truthfulness, the difficulty of which I do not minimize, arises
from the ability to affirm the ambivalences that pretense would
conceal. Whereas lies endlessly diminish the relevant data,
truthfulness seeks to embrace ever more accurately whatever
has been one's life. In pursuit of greater integration of the
parts of a life, truthfulness ignores progressively less of one's
past.

Pretense is central to the effort to avoid faith. Although a
pretender may appear to be pious, such piety seeks to gain

approval by selectively emphasizing certain aspects of a life. In this it seeks also to avoid risks and change. *Only when life is recognized as inescapably risky does the urgency of faith begin to be evident.* America's aversion to ambiguity is but one of the notable ways in which we avoid embracing life-as-risk. Those who seek the truth about themselves undertake the great risk because there is so much about every life needing to be forgiven in order that it may be affirmed. Forgiveness is the precondition for that which truth-seeking people may affirm about their lives. To be forgiven is, contrary to a popular maxim, to be able to see all; forgiveness, thus, is key to the reclamation of one's life.

The ability to be truthful is not a natural virtue. Naturally, we tend to conceal and misrepresent. One of our misrepresentations is about knowledge itself, when it is suggested that to know all is to forgive all. Increasingly I doubt that there is any causal connection at all between knowing and forgiving. Whoever suggested an inner connection between them apparently misread his or her experience. Knowledge may open our eyes, but we still may not see with compassion. Knowledge enables exploitation at least as readily as it does forgiveness. The distinctive biblical understanding turns these realities inside out: it is forgiveness that enables us to see what we are naturally unable to recognize about ourselves. Truth is not just something "out there"; it is always subject to inner qualities as well. It is those qualities that are put right by God's forgiveness. When we are freed of the fear of consequences, we are able to be more truthful about our own experiences. The process of reclaiming the long-ignored past begins with the forgiveness which encourages us to remember. Although I suspect that this order is the dynamic of the work of self-recovery, that assured forgiveness frees memory, I am uncomfortable with claiming any finality for such an order of events. Since nobody can prove anything about this realm where so much that is very important is found, I prefer greater imprecision. It seems to me quite possible that a person could remember all too vividly certain disturbing events in his or her own past. Much such recollection is clearly self-destructive:

the person may be incapable of either benefiting from or getting free of particular memories. One tune plays on endlessly. That person forgiven will, without abandoning the punitive old tune, be able to subdue it by making it but one of many recallable events.

The function of forgiveness in these settings is to liberate people trapped in partial recollection. Unlike drugs or lobotomy, forgiveness does not obliterate memories. Rather, by deflating the "monstrous" memory, by humanizing that which the ill person has enlarged beyond all hope, forgiveness enables him or her to incorporate such memories into present self-understanding. The effect of this is to give the forgiven person access to energies that were previously deployed in resisting the monsters. Thus is forgiveness the means by which a previously imprisoned person is liberated for good works. Forgiveness remains a gracious mystery beyond human control, yet the yearnings of the person in bondage are intrinsic to the process by which eyes are opened to see more than was previously possible, or to see the well-recalled past in a more healing light. Whether the result is an enlarged or less punitive memory, the ingredients that I feel unable to arrange in the necessary order are God's grace and human initiative. I cannot escape the suspicion that the interworking of these dynamics are to be reverenced but, probably, never finally explained.

EXPOSING NEGATIVE ATTITUDES

We turn now from prologue to discussion of the question underlying the chapter title: In what sense, if at all, are we able to speak of aging as part of God's purpose for human lives? Since not all people live long enough to be aware of the process of growing older, it cannot be an absolutely necessary experience. God has other ways of awakening men and women short of advanced age. The question for us, however, is what spiritual maturation might be hoped for in life's last decades. And what do we know about the processes of such maturation?

As should have been clear from my earlier approaches to such questions—for example, the suggestion of an *indirect* approach to one's autobiography—I resist the temptation to answer these questions directly. My refusal so to prescribe the content of later life's spirituality or to identify the steps toward such maturation, a refusal which will irritate those who desire simple, clear, "religious" answers, arises from all I have said about society's profound influence on what may be aging's vocation from God. That this influence is almost wholly negative is the conclusion to which I have reluctantly come. Whereas in many societies aging is a cause for pride and a source of beauty, with us growing older is at least a matter of embarrassment and a cause for spiritually debilitating dishonesty. Nothing good can come from being deceptive, and it is rare that embarrassment leads to appropriate affirmation. At the least, though this is bad enough, others are deceived about us; at the worst, we come to believe our own lies.

An informed affirmation of one's life and one's times—a long-term assignment in which one both draws upon and deepens one's love for neighbor and self to the glory of God—is central to older people's witness. Our first responsibility, therefore, is to recognize some of the important ways in which societal attitudes and values both discourage and encourage this work. It will not do to have in mind a program for elders while ignoring the social forces constantly working against our design. For that program to have any chance of prevailing, we must be utterly clear about what needs to be offset and the societal resources that may be available. What constitutes human aging's somewhat distinctive work will become clear in the process of identifying and deflating social attitudes inimical to the realities of growing older. In my understanding it is impossible to prescribe for all people in all social settings one normative program. The first step to enable individuals to determine their distinctive work is to identify and combat contrary public attitudes by which all who wish to act their age are adversely affected. To hold that aging is God's plan must not be confused with the belief in a nonexistent blueprint that would tell everybody how to age. People are alike only in their need to recognize how particular attitudes may hinder or help their maturation. It is to those tasks of identification that we now turn.

In Chapter 4, the work of self-acquaintance of which we spoke was largely internal. Nothing that follows contradicts that, but the focus changes somewhat. In order to plan for our later years as men and women of faith, we must look discerningly and continually at the society into which we were born and by which we were largely shaped. We must become more aware of the attitudes and values to which we have unthinkingly assented. In the interest of a vocation for our later years we need to distance ourselves from many of these.

Attitudes and values may have been formed so subtly and accepted so widely, at least in circles with which we have been familiar, as to have been unrecognized. Indeed, for a long time we probably thought that it was universal reality which we perceived through our inherited outlook and prescribed behavior. Such is the consequence of every parochialism. After long struggle with our societal outlook, I have concluded that at least four attitudes have long been dominant in my experience. Further, I am convinced that they are inimical to the work of the later years. That is why identifying them—giving them names, as Jesus named the demons—is the necessary first step in putting them in their proper, nondominating place. Although these attitudes may have been functional during those decades in which success was the goal and the multiple obligations of family, career, and citizenship were inescapable, they are progressively less so when we are searching for fulfillment. To repeat Jung's insistence: life's afternoon may not be lived according to the agenda of the morning. Activities once appropriate or unavoidable, elements of which endure to the end of life, become more marginal and less compelling.[2] Outlooks change.

To put it perhaps too bluntly, we are as Christians discouraged from following what may be God's agenda for the later years by attitudes commonly held in this society. I hesitate to identify my hunches about appropriate developments for the later years of our lives as God's agenda for two reasons. First, people are different. I have little desire to prescribe one program for all. Second, because there is so little guidance in Scripture, especially in the New Testament, we simply do not know for sure what God intends for those who are privileged to live into advanced years. The extent of longevity in the late twentieth century is unique. It may be the most significant demographic change in history. Although there have always been isolated cases of individuals who lived long, the situation is dramatically changed when generations of cohorts may expect to do so. Nobody knows quite what the change does or should mean for the society. It is partly for this reason that it is important for the churches to attempt to raise the questions that society would repress. Perhaps the best we can do is to share our limited understandings this way in the hope that, through the variety of people in local churches who willingly grapple with these issues and their own experiences, the Spirit will instruct us about the ingredients of those wise hearts for which the poet prayed to God (see Psalm 90:12).

The four attitudes that make it difficult to get onto whatever may be God's agenda for the later years are these: (1) the importance of being in *control*; (2) the desire to hold the *initiative*; (3) the priority placed on the ability *to produce and consume*, which we call "adulthood" and (4) the assumption that there are *answers to all questions*. However, these attitudes, when properly understood, are among the resources for approaching one's later years. But they need to be identified anew. Because they have influenced most of our behaviors to date, and in light of changes discussed in the previous chapter, we need to reconsider the importance we attach to them. Such value as inheres in these attitudes, and it is considerable, is compromised to the extent that we insist upon their enduring *centrality* to our self-understanding. They serve us better when their sway in our lives is less than absolute.

Let me illustrate by exploring the last of these attitudes somewhat more fully. My comments might equally well apply to the imperiousness of the other three.

Undergirded by the other three—the need to be in control, the belief that some initiative is always possible, and, supported by daily media reassurances, the belief that there is a purchase that will take care of our problems—we are impatient when confronted by unanswered questions. They imply an impotence which we abhor. In large part we respond to such restlessness by concentrating our attention on questions to which answers can be found. These tend to be quantitative and within the capability of a society of engineers. The problem for the later years is that such information is decreasingly useful. At some point in the lives of most people quite different questions begin to emerge. They have to do with quality rather than quantities, such as, What is the meaning of life? On what basis have I achieved or neglected what I have? To what kind of society have I contributed? What have I done that is useful for others? Am I satisfied with the quality of my relationships? Have I been neglectful of my inner life? What inner life do I actually have? Why am I often overcome with regrets? Have I understood well enough the involvement of my life with people far removed and often unknown? Have I recognized the extent to which my life has been determined? Have I let myself be deceived about the extent to which I have been in control? Have I possibly proceeded on a cluster of assumptions that were never as adequate as I and others pretended? Why have I been plagued with resentment toward others? Have I faced the fact of my own mortality? Is there time to get in touch with the operative realities rather than the pretenses of my life? If so, am I motivated to do so?

These are the questions which Paul Gauguin, at an early age, must have often asked himself before abandoning his bourgeois life for a different one in Tahiti: "Whence come? What are we? Whither go we?" Few will react as dramatically as he; few permanently escape the questions. John Steinbeck put them in yet another way: "Have I lived enough? Have I loved enough?"

To such questions there are no easy answers. That is part of what keeps many from recognizing their importance. Behind this fact, however, is the societal aversion to the unanswerable. We are ill-prepared to live with such questions.

This determination to avoid them is especially punishing for the aged. Two responses are commonplace: either denial of the questions in a continuing pretense that, because one still acts young, the questions have not surfaced; or deepening depression about the questions themselves and about one's inability to embrace and be nurtured by them. I would not undervalue either the reality of the questions or the real difficulty in knowing how to respond to them. Probably most older people have found themselves so confronted. The point is to emphasize the nonproductive *anguish caused to older people by negative societal attitudes toward both the aging and to the questions that age often generates.* Could it be that such ageist attitudes result less from the uncertainty about what to do with the aging than from frustration with the unanswerable questions often raised by older people? Are we not often similarly impatient with adolescents' questions? Questions of purpose and quality uncover uncertainties which "adults" prefer to ignore. Better, we say, to be able to do something with simpler questions than to be immobilized by hard ones.

To recognize that there are some things that one *can* do is clearly a positive ingredient in all human experience. The possibility may be as simple as being able to swallow water from a glass held in a nurse's hand. However, there often comes a time in the course of growing older when there are even harder things to swallow—unanswerable questions that people wish we would not ask. This is the double bind: being unable to suppress those questions appropriate to one's age in which others are definitely not interested. How better to assure, as we often do with adolescents, that the questioner is kept in isolation and uncertainty? But, whereas youth may break out of the impasse by taking on the frenzied activity of adulthood, such is no longer an option for those whose active years have passed. In many lives this lack of action is less a matter of deficient energy than of experience-acquired skepticism about what action may accomplish. Yet more important is older persons' unwillingness to suppress the questions. Knowing the folly of such concealment, they intuit the significance of the unanswerable.

IDENTIFYING POSITIVE EXPERIENCES

Having noted some of the widely held attitudes that discourage older people from searching out and working at the agenda appropriate to their stage of life, we must identify certain experiences which may assist them in that work. In doing this, we must remember two things. First, the attitudes we have just described are enduringly powerful. They do not cease to exercise control over us simply by being labeled. They have been for too long intrinsic to our self-understanding to be so easily overcome. Second, and paradoxically, most of the needed resources lie hidden within the outlooks we have mentioned. That they are not easily accessible results from the single-mindedness with which society exhorts us to have control and initiative, to accept popular imagery, and to insist on answers. The very consistency and volume with which we are so exhorted suggests that something important is being hidden. That what is being suppressed is important to elders is my suspicion. That the concealed might be revealed is the task to which we now turn.

In my experience it has long been evident that there are no unchanging answers to the sorts of questions we have been asking: "Have I lived enough? Have I loved enough?" At every stage of life some form of these questions and others like them are asked and answered. They do not necessarily come to mind as consciously as we are here raising them. Nor do they arise as consciously as we ask other questions, such as, Shall we buy a house, or rent? Where shall I go to college? Shall I contribute to this appeal? If so, how much? However, in answering the questions of which we are more aware we have also been answering Gauguin's questions: Whence, What, and Whither. Oscar Wilde's *Picture of Dorian Gray* tells a story—more graphically than most people actually recognize in their experience—of the inner changes that occurred unavoidably as a man indulged his desires uncritically. For the highly moral purposes of the story, Dorian Gray's deterioration was recorded only in the self-portrait concealed from all eyes but his own. His eventual disgust with the consequences of his consistent self-indulgence is what makes this tale a modern morality piece. That Gray finally took his own life illustrates the despair to which some people may be driven by discovering what their lives have actually been—and their consequences. Many older people reverse an attitude of their earlier years: what they know about themselves becomes more important than what others perceive.

Few have such a vivid, visual reminder of the cumulative inner consequences of the way they have long been answering basic questions as did Dorian Gray. But the cumulative evidence of how we have lived exists, and it is part of the process of aging to recognize how we have *actually* made choices and invested energy. That the process of self-recognition often begins earlier may well explain why life's middle years are so traumatic for many. We are able, finally, to recognize patterns of preference which have been operative in our lives and to face their undeniable and not necessarily unpleasant consequences. At some point, most people discover that they have lived out the advice given by Rilke to the young poet who pleaded for answers.

> Try to love the *questions themselves* . . . [answers] cannot be given you because you would not be able to live them. And the point is to live everything. *Live* the questions now. *Perhaps you will then gradually, without noticing it, live along some distant day into the answer.* [emphasis added][3]

Whether or not we like the answer we find at the "distant day," and what to do if we do not, is part of the burden with which age must come to terms. The ability to recognize the inherent nobility of this task is the direction in which society must move. Hard questions are not demeaning.

What is recorded in our lives is in consequence of many choices. How we have chosen to invest ourselves, or to withhold from involvement, may not be inferred from a single episode or even a cluster of events. *Over time, however, one acts as one is;* or, one chooses on the basis of previous covert answers, often unconsciously held, to life's hard questions. For at least one thing aging enables us: to begin to identify these preference patterns. To cite Burns again, it is the power of aging to give us the gift "to see ourselves as others see us!" The gains foreseen by the poet could be vast:

It wad frae mony a blunder free us,
  And foolish notion:
What airs in dress and gait wad lea'e us
  And ev'n devotion![4]

Perhaps because of the outcome of Wilde's story I have given
the wrong impression of what people actually find. Few are
like Dorian Gray, uncovering only the no-longer-ignorable
decay of their lives. Some discover beauty and connectedness
which, because of their modesty, others may not have recognized earlier. These are men and women whose lives have long
been quietly centering; certainly they are those who, by valuing their own incompleteness, have acted on an acknowledged
and treasured relationship with people and with the natural
world. Others, as Wilde insists, find only ugliness and alienation. In the language of Erik Erikson, some older lives are
marked by integrity, others possessed by despair and self-
disgust.

Most lives fall into neither extreme. When self-recognition
becomes possible, most of us discover both elements of integrity
and grounds for despair. Could it be otherwise? This is the
starting point for identifying aging's agenda: recognition of
the accumulated evidence of one's life. We have been answering
life's hard questions all along! Without that acknowledgement,
no further growth is possible. For those who refuse to recognize
the evidence, the answer to our fundamental question is
straightforward: it *is* for nothing that they have grown older.
They continue to exist without living.

To admit the evidence does not assure willingness to undertake whatever growth may be possible. Such willingness will
itself be the consequence of whatever prior risky personal
growth one has ventured. We are dealing here with a kind of
iron law—courage and faintheartedness breed their kind.
Much as we might wish otherwise, we are confronted by one of
the hardest truths of the New Testament: "For to those who
have, more will be given; and from those who have nothing,
even what they have will be taken away" (Mark 4:25). The
exhortation to generosity of spirit, which is the context for this
text, is predictive.

One of the major achievements possible in the process of growing old is to recognize the answers to difficult questions which have gradually taken shape in the course of answering a myriad of seemingly less important questions. To a far greater extent than is ordinarily recognized, whom we have become is the inevitable consequence of choices we have made. That that iron law need not be the last word is the insistence to which we must now turn.

IMAGES OF RESISTANCE AND AFFIRMATION

Our relationship with God may mature through such a process of self-acquaintance. With fewer illusions about being self-made or about our purity of heart—that is, if we are clearer about the *actual* history and present condition of our life—either we will be driven to deeper despair or God will become ever more completely God for us. Apart from remaining incorrigibly ignorant about ourselves, there is no alternative to the dangers and promise inherent in the process of self-acquaintance. In the last analysis, the double discovery of our indebtedness and of our mixed character is the experience out of which God may become our God. By becoming ever more ourselves, by discovering how far from "home" we have strayed—as the "lost sheep" in the General Confession insists we are—we may see the home for which we have since the beginning been destined. St. Augustine discovered that he had always been in the home from which he long thought he had fled.

In his *Confessions*, written after he had been a bishop for years, Augustine recalled the decades of his brilliant and erratic life in which he sought widely for any personal grounding other than the Christian faith of his mother Monica. With his brilliant intellect and good eye for promising opportunities, he would have been a "success" in almost any environment or time. These skills took him all the way to the top of his career as a rhetorician. A sensuous man, unable to confine his lust to his common-law wife of fifteen years, he relished the pleasures of the flesh in which he readily indulged. Like many bright undergraduates, he luxuriated in intellectual and sexual activ-

ity.. It was almost the perfect combination and, as he long
thought, free of the inelegance and constraints of Monica's
God.

Almost, but not quite!

Long-suppressed indebtedness to his parents, friends, and
teachers were still within the man. Gradually some of the
inhumanity of his treatment of those who had meant most to
him—simple things like teasing a mortally ill friend about his
baptism, abandoning his mother in pursuit of private ambitions—were seen for what they were. Through these involuntary awarenesses the self-styled academician/sensualist was in
the process of preparing for his later years.

How all this story unfolded is readily accessible in Augustine's autobiography, the first such book ever written.[5] The
point is that God became the gracious God for Augustine only
as he was able to acknowledge actually who he had become.
His life-transforming discovery was that, contrary to his long-
held assumption, God had always been present to his life.
There was nothing more to it than his glad acknowledgment of
this graceful reality.

There were, of course, important losses in the process. They
were for him real but incomparable with his gains. How all
this worked out in the balance of Augustine's long career as
bishop, author of a host of publications, defender of the faith,
is a story the interested reader may profitably pursue. For the
purpose of thinking about the self-acquaintance which may be
integral to the work of one's later years, a good beginning is to
start reading his *Confessions*, the most important Christian
composition after the New Testament canon.

Like Augustine, what we need are images which empower in
two directions. Negatively, they need to be able to identify and
resist the societal pressures that urge continued allegiance to
the sorts of attitudes that characterized his life prior to his
conversion. The pressures to conform in these ways are formidable: they mandate that we retain control, continue with
initiatives, produce/consume, and frame our questions so that
answers are possible. We cannot know how powerful these
assumptions are until the first time we question their ade-

quacy for the later years. So to challenge prevailing attitudes will reveal in others, often those to whom we thought ourselves closest, how close to the surface ageist attitudes really are. In this society the prudent person will ask such questions with the greatest discretion—if at all.

But Christians may not be equated with prudence. As I tried to suggest in the title of my first book, we are called to live *Against the Grain*. I elaborated this characterization of the people of faith in a chapter of another book, *Looking Both Ways: A Theology for Mid-Life*.[6] There I designated the church as "Community of Support and Defiance." Central to our vocation is the obligation to name and resist evil where and when we encounter it. Society's antipathy to whatever may be aging's proper agenda is, for me, such an evil. We need images that will encourage efforts to expose and to defy this evil.

Beyond this important work, however, our images must have positive benefits. Once free, or in the process of being freed, from constraining societal attitudes we need encouragement to get on with the discovery of what may be our proper agenda for life's later years. Thus, the images that we revere and ponder must empower us both to resist others' expectations for us, however well-meaning, and to affirm those realizations which will occur to us and our cohorts as we seek to understand what it might mean that God has allowed us to live so long. In such efforts to become what we really are, to be accountable for what we are actually able to make of our later years, God becomes God for us.

This, then, is the double work of those who would affirm aging as God's design: to expose and restrict social attitudes of gradually diminishing importance and to discover together some of the marks of God's image for those in life's later years. They will become both wiser about their personal experience and more discerning about how things have changed, often for the worse, in the society. Like Augustine, they will gradually discover that God has never been far from either personal or public life.

Having thus gathered themselves together, they will be men and women fiercely alive for the sake of the quality of the future. That they may well not live to enjoy any reforms of public life matters less than that, at the moment, they stand somewhere between memory and hope in what they know to be a *living* present.

Whereas selective inattention to aspects of one's being may be functional in achieving limited goals earlier in life, aging's design requires us to move beyond such selectivity. Greater comprehensiveness of self-understanding is aging's concluding assignment: to lay claim both to the life that we have lived and the life we have neglected. As we begin to affirm this as a good design for living, it becomes ever more persuasively God's design.

Epilogue

"When at last age has assembled you together, will it not be easy to let it all go, lived, balanced, over?"[1] If the answer implied by Florida Scott-Maxwell, a Jungian therapist in her ninth decade, is positive, there is no necessary discontinuity between life and death. Whether or not that ability "to let it all go" is anybody's experience, I do not know. Ms. Scott-Maxwell's conditions for such relinquishment will probably elude most people. Which of us is likely to be satisfied with the adequacy of how we have lived, how well balanced have been our efforts? In greater likelihood we will be plagued with guilt and regrets and/or an insatiable desire for yet more living. So wrote a thoughtful friend recently: "The longer I live the more I want. I feel assembled now—at last—and I'm finding that this now is about the best—some wisdom accumulated over the years, enjoyment of nostalgia, wonderfully varied work to do."

Although I am inclined to value discontinuity as in this instance she does not, I must acknowledge my feeling that Ms. Scott-Maxwell may have described life's end as it *should* be. Of course, her assumption is that we will have so lived that age will be able to assemble us together. That aging might have such a positive function is problematic on at least two counts. First, as we have contended throughout this book, our ageist attitudes hardly include such a constructive role for growing older. Second, aging's ability to accomplish a sense of integrity rather than despair presupposes years of paying attention to one's experience. Such extended reflection, itself little encour-

aged today, could make possible such a centering in one's final
years. So centered, it might then be possible "to let it all go." I
doubt, however, that it will ever be easy.

The possibility of such ultimate relinquishment arises from
a well-established awareness of the inescapable reality of gains
and losses in all human experience. Any final continuity between life and death is made possible by innumerable previous
discontinuities gladly embraced. Since these real losses, which
everybody suffers, trigger questions about one's faith, it is to
this understanding of the inseparability of gains and losses
that I turn first. A grasp of this inseparability would seem to
be the precondition for any likelihood that growing older may
serve to assemble us together. It is the temptation to separate
gains from losses that Christian faith may also enable us to
resist.

My governing assumption is that the central issue in aging,
as was equally true in earlier years, is the faith question, *Can
I trust God in view of the uncertainties of life's next stage?* Such
trust translates into the ability to believe in the adequacy of
my God-given capabilities to make some sense of the risks
involved in each stage of potential growth. What is universal
about human development is less its described patterns than
the fact that each of us must draw upon our distinctive resources to affirm life's challenges.

On this assumption let us look at a short paragraph from a
compelling historical record. Among the experiences of men
and women en route to the last frontier of the American West,
Francis Parkman recorded the following:

> It is worth noticing that on the Platte one may sometimes
> see the shattered wrecks of ancient claw-footed tables,
> well-waxed and rubbed, or massive bureaus of carved oak
> . . . brought, perhaps originally from England; then, with
> the declining fortunes of their owners, borne across the
> Alleghanies to the wilderness of Ohio or Kentucky; then
> to Illinois or Missouri; and now at last fondly stowed away
> in the family wagon for the interminable journey to Ore-
> gon. But the stern privations of the way are little antici-

pated. The cherished relic is soon flung out to scorch and crack upon the hot prairie.[2]

Circumstances rarely allow one to carry all of the external accumulations from one stage of life to another. In no way is this to suggest that it is ever easy to abandon cherished possessions; who we are, or think we are, is often seemingly inseparable from what we own.

Parkman's description of furniture abandoned along the Platte River is a compelling parable of universal human experience: that losses are inseparable from gains as one moves through all of life's stages. If we concentrate only on the valued possessions that had to be left behind, we lose sight of the reason for their abandonment. *Things were jettisoned in the westward trek in order that the settlers might reach a desired destination.* It is unlikely that many foresaw the hardship to which they would be subject en route to their opportunity for new life. They did not anticipate that getting there would require lightening the load with which they boldly set out from Missouri, but we distort their experience if we are preoccupied only with their diminishments. Those were real, but they were in the interest of an envisioned greater good. That there are unavoidable losses in the progress from one stage of life to the next is one of the fundamental facts to which American eyes are often closed. Is there any way back to childhood innocence? Or to the turbulence and uncertain grandiosity of adolescence? Or, in later years, to the vigor and illusions of middle age? In achieving the gains of maturity, as in reaching the Oregonian destination, some things have had to be relinquished along the way. *To believe in the living God is to be willing to live in the present,* whatever furniture needs to be discarded. To affirm present life is to teeter willingly between memory and hope, refusing to let either the claims of the past or the possibilities of the future ever determine the living present. Most often the temptation is to hold on too long to the past. Although there may be few things more beguiling than an innocent infant or more attractive than a maturing adolescent, is anything less attractive or less appropriate than a mid-life adolescent?

Shakespeare certainly disapproved of such immaturity in the words he wrote for the newly crowned King Henry V. Falstaff, jolly companion of his days as the fun-loving Prince Hal, had greeted him thus, "God save thee, my sweet boy, my King, my Jove." To this suggestion that nothing had changed, Henry replied:

> I know thee not, old man: fall to thy prayers;
> How ill white hairs become a fool and jester!
> I have long dreamed of such a kind of man,
> So surfeit-swelled, so old and so profane;
> But, being awaked, I do despise my dream.
> Make less they body hence, and more thy grace;
> Leave gormandizing; know the grave doth gape
> For thee thrice wider than for other men,
> Reply not to me with a fool-born jest:
> Presume not that I am the thing I was;
> For God doth know, so shall the world perceive,
> That I have turned away my former self;
> So will I those that kept me company.[3]

"Presume not that I am the thing I was." Although there is an indestructible continuity to all lives, we do not remain what we have been. Without anything as dramatic as an ascent to the throne to change us, we both are not and are today the persons we were yesterday. Such are the dynamics of our lives and the source of challenge to our faith.

This emphasis on the inseparability of gains and losses should not be interpreted as a preference for one stage of life over the others. I do not suggest that one period of life is more inherently "religious" than the others. Rather, *on the assumption that the passages from birth to death are God's ordinary means of calling us to relationship by calling us to be ourselves, every stage involves the faith question.* Do we trust God that it will make sense to give up present security for the sake of the greater promise? Are we able to trust the adequacy of our God-given resources to move us on to life's next stage? In aging the questions recur. Such uncertainty is not new for us. In every transitional passage we have been so challenged.

Having emphasized that the ability to affirm the awareness of the inescapability of gains and losses is the direct consequence of belief in the *living* God, and having suggested that we are brought into relationship with God—the decisive relationship of *human* life—by getting ever more deeply in touch with our own particular lives, we are able to see the distinctive reason for belonging to inclusive fellowships. It is not simply that, like a herd of animals, we may have company and protection. More central is the conviction that we need the widest variety of other people in order to get in touch with *the variety of characters within each of us*. We are not self-made. It is by learning to love the range of "personae" within, which means, at the least, to acknowledge our distinctive complexity, that we develop our sense of kinship with all sorts and conditions of men and women. Because, no matter our age, there remains within each of us a helpless infant and a hopeful but sometimes frightened child, and it is in this way that we know our kinship with the young. Because there is an aged one within us, no matter how chronologically old we are, we have evidence of kinship with even the eldest among us. Such self-awareness, which is an aspect of the self-love to which Jesus exhorts us, is the key to our ability to love our neighbors of all ages and conditions.

At no time between birth and death are we ever just what we may appear to be: a beguiling or fractious child, a promising or troubled adolescent, a vigorous young adult, a self-confident person in mid-life, a wise and possibly somewhat withdrawn older man or woman. At any given time we can be at only one of these stages. Equally important, however, is the fact that all of the other stages are present either as memory or as anticipated potentialities. There is always a *configuration* of ingredients; their vividness depends strictly on our ability to remember and to foresee. At any given time only some of these ingredients will appropriately be the central preoccupation, but the other inner characters, temporarily peripheral, contain additional God-given resources for present tasks. To be willing to stand in the "living present" is our vocation, but this requires an awareness that there is always more to us than these immediate challenges to growth. To be alive to the widest range of present opportunities and obligations is to evidence faith in the *living* God; there is no way in faith to escape the vulnerability of such a stance. The point, however, is that we will be able to embrace such risk to the extent that we have learned from others that there is more to each of us than the self which we immediately present to the world.

That there is something more to us than is ordinarily recognized, or than we ourselves acknowledge, tempts and frightens us. Where fear prevails we often seek refuge by embracing ever more tightly some of the roles appropriate earlier in life. We hope for invulnerability by pretending that such retreat is both possible and desirable. It is not, however, in flight to the past that our vocation is to be found. Such rejection of both present and future assures only the boredom and fatigue of a progressively diminished world.

Engagement with life, and the energy that issues from such connectedness, requires us to affirm rather than reject, to be vulnerable in hope rather than self-protective in fear. It is a striking contemporary paradox that many people become free to discover their vocation and embrace its uncertainties and demands only after they retire. Such are the pulls to the past that even then such discovery is not assured. Like the merchant who found the pearl of great price, we have to be on the lookout for treasure, or at least vaguely aware that there must be something better than the consumer-oriented life, and willing to risk all to acquire it. (See Matthew 13:45f.) For such risk taking to be possible, something significant must have changed. (The merchant's eyes must have been opened to the greater value of some things over others.) For many contemporary people, their work will have to end in order for them to be able to recognize their calling. This distinction between work and calling may come as a shock to those who have long equated job with vocation.

In an essay for a theological wordbook, I wrote, "Popular employment of the word [vocation] to cover any person's work represents the complete emptying of its original content."[4] That article emphasized a possible relationship between calling and work. It is that relationship that current misuse of the word "vocation" obscures. We speak of a person's vocation as though it had no reference to anything other than the work done. While virtually all work that serves human need *may* afford opportunity for giving expression to one's calling, that vocation is prior to and must be distinguished from a job.

It is God who calls men and women into that relationship which we identify as faith. It is God who would engender in humans that ultimate trust which frees them to acknowledge the range and complexity of their God-givenness. It is from within such a faith that the courage to affirm one's cumbersome wholeness arises. There is much more to every person than is ordinarily acknowledged. Especially in our work, though not exclusively there, we learn to value only those aspects of our God-givenness which are there functional. On this constricted self-presentation, which all too easily and for too long becomes one's total self-understanding, there is no way for aging to assemble anybody together as Scott-Maxwell imagines. A significant change must occur whereby one is gradually reacquainted with neglected aspects of one's givenness. For many people this becomes possible only as they move, or are moved, beyond the confined and confining roles that they pretended were adequate for their complete self-expression. It is a liberating article of the biblical faiths that there is more to becoming human than what one does in the world. The work we do may express a self-understanding as made in God's image. In no way, however, is that something-more-than-our-competencies ever equatable with our job. There is always more to who we are than either we grasp or allow others to see. Who we are becoming in God's image may be related to, but is never derivable from, what we do. Whether we know ourselves, or would be known, by the what or the who of our lives, makes, literally, a world of difference.

This life-saving discovery is made by some people at their retirement. Others do so at some other time when they come to embrace the positive potential inherent in aging. Nothing assures that this rather than the potential for despair will be experienced. In a society which attaches the importance we do to work and the "success" that it makes possible, it will be impossible—at least initially—for some people to move beyond the work roles from which they have been retired. Despair over the loss of a career is probably more likely for people who have been effectively persuaded to value only certain aspects of their God-givenness. Such inability to become more and, in part, other than one has been—such attachment to the past—dictates against Scott-Maxwell's expectation that it will be possible to "let it all go."

As the words of Dylan Thomas stridently and perhaps inadvertently emphasize, "Go not gentle into that good night," those who have allowed themselves to be confinedly misrepresented cannot let go. I find these words, written at the time of his father's death, at least as revealing of his own condition as of his grief. While I sometimes admire his heroic defiance and would not be thought to be urging premature passivity, I think Thomas misses the point. Struggle, which is inescapable, is no where more important than in the desire to be connected with ever more of our God-givenness. Averse to passivity and responding to his father's death, the poet provides a counterbalance to Scott-Maxwell's sanguinity. That a half century separated their ages, to say nothing of their significantly dissimilar temperaments, may help explain their quite different approaches to life's end. The rage expressed by Thomas I find too sophomoric; Scott-Maxwell's attractive vision takes too little account of the high price of self-acquaintance to be paid before one is able to "let it all go."

There is much to rage against long before the night of Dylan Thomas's poem. Opportunities for heroism may lead to more irenic attitudes toward death than was possible for the indulgent young poet. Moving as he was in alcoholism into ever narrower self-acquaintance, it is not surprising that he clung desperately to that which he was in the process of destroying. There is a world of difference between a life slipping like sand through one's fingers, as was his, and an assembled life. What looks like cowardice through his eyes, may to Scott-Maxwell be a final relinquishment of God-given complexity long maintained. None of us makes faultless use of our varied gifts. It is for this reason that our vocation from God is crucial. In that calling we are free to return to its Perfect Source all of our avoidable imperfection. It will never be "balanced" but, in faith, we will be able to acknowledge initially that it was the life we lived. Beyond that our vocation will be recognized in the repeated insistence that there is more to me than I ever recognized. We emerge from mystery and, in faith, a gracious mystery is our destiny.

Aging makes such self-recognition possible to the extent that we learn to refuse to be equated with life's unavoidably confined roles. As we come to realize that, in our God-givenness, we are not so reducible we may learn to cling less desperately to what we can now see was only part of what we truly are.

It is only when we are taxed beyond our ordinary ability to cope with our lives—for example, only when we willingly confront the different perspectives of those who share our humanity—that there is the possibility that God may become God for us. Such faith may be known only when, recognizing the need for resources beyond those by which we ordinarily keep life under control, we assent to the vulnerability and loss for the sake of the potential gains. Such moments can occur in the widest range of settings: for example, when we attempt to see life through the eyes of a child or a spouse, or when told that we are terminally ill. This is the radical faith context in which we must think about the importance of inclusive community. Although there are faith avoiders within the churches, there are also people at each of life's stages who are risk takers. They are discovering God-as-God for themselves as they learn to trust the adequacy of their God-given particulars. In no way is this to claim the total adequacy of their God-givenness. This we claim only for the Messiah. However, if any one of us is to be capable of doing any good in the world, it will be on the basis of our assent to our God-givenness. Each person has only some gifts; each is a combination of strengths *and* weaknesses. This is no cause for embarrassment or concealment. It is by glad assent to the actualities of our lives—by self-love—that we are on the road to effective neighbor-love.

Such assent begins for me with the acknowledgment that I am somewhere along the time line between the cradle and the grave. By this acknowledgment I admit to a certain amount of experience and to at least some curiosity about that of those who are older. It means also that certain questions are especially urgent at present. Although I am quite willing to listen to what perplexes others and to respond as I am able, I am also hoping for their comparably attentive responses to my perplexities. It is not answers, or even advice, that we have for each other. Rather, we have the God-derived ability to encourage each other to honor our questions and to begin to trust the adequacy of our particular abilities to live into our own "answers" to such questions. This is the material of Christian life together; where such issues are posed and attention paid to them, there is Christ present. So I understand the assurance to any two or three gathered in his name (see Matthew 18:20). Such a gathering is for no purpose initially other than to acknowledge our fear of and fascination with the inescapable faith questions. By that candor we may encourage each other to undertake the risks for the sake of the gains inherent in being present to the present. That there will be losses we have acknowledged; that there will be gains from such intentional life is the nature of God's promise to be God for us. Faith's work is always to encourage us to be present to ourselves. So connected to ourselves in an inclusive community, people provide assurances to each other that are often persuasive. In such a setting, is it so farfetched to suggest that age may finally assemble us together? In the meantime, we cannot be but more vividly alive!

Notes

Chapter 1

1. David J. Maitland, *Aging: A Time for New Learning* (Louisville: The Westminster/John Knox Press, 1987).

2. David J. Maitland, *Against the Grain: Coming Through Midlife Crisis* (New York: Pilgrim Press, 1981).

3. William Shakespeare, *As You Like It*, Act 2, Sc. 7, lines 167–176 (New York: Washington Square Press, 1959).

4. Florida Scott-Maxwell, *The Measure of My Days* (New York: Alfred A. Knopf, 1968), 42.

5. Ibid.

6. Ken Dychtwald and Joe Flower, who have recently published *Age Wave* (New York: Tarcher, 1989), are welcome exceptions to my generalization.

7. Maitland, *Against the Grain*, p. 11f.

8. Marcus Tullius Cicero, "Of Death and Old Age," in *Middle Age, Old Age*, ed. Ruth G. Lyell, (New York: Harcourt, Brace Jovanovich, 1980), 307ff.

9. *Minneapolis Star Tribune*, 30 January 1988.

Chapter 2

1. Hugo Young, "Commentary," *The Guardian*, 11 June 1987.

2. C. G. Jung, *Memories, Dreams, Reflections* (New York: Random House, Inc., 1961), 144.

3. For an extended discussion of the relationship of articles of the Apostles Creed to the variety of human experience, see David J. Maitland, *Looking Both Ways* (Louisville: Westminster/John Knox Press, 1985), especially Chapter 4 on Christology.

4. Bill Holm, *The Music of Failure* (Marshall, Minn.: Plains Press, 1985), 12.

5. Dag Hammarskjöld, *Markings*, trans. Leif Sjoberg (New York: Alfred A. Knopf, 1967), 84.

6. For further discussion of some of the very important personal disclosures in his journal see chapter 7, "Self-hate, Self-love, Self-denial," in *Looking Both Ways*.

7. For discussion of the interrelationships of the loves in Jesus' summary of the Law, see David J. Maitland, *Against the Grain: Coming Through Mid-life Crisis* (New York: Pilgrim Press, 1981).

8. Nicholas Monsarrat, *The Cruel Sea* (New York: Alfred A. Knopf, 1951).

9. Tom Stoppard, *The Observer*, 28 June 1987.

10. Harold H. Ditmanson, "Hours of Authority," *St. Olaf*, 36 (June-July 1988): 3.

Chapter 3

1. C. J. Jung, *Modern Man in Search of a Soul* (New York: Harcourt, Brace, Jovanavich, 1933), 108.

2. Ronald Blythe, *Akenfield: Portrait of an English Village* (London: Allen Lane, 1969).

3. See 1 Corinthians 12:15ff regarding the self-sufficiency which denies its need for other parts.

4. E. B. White, *The Second Tree from the Corner* (New York: Harper & Brothers, 1954).

5. Margaret Todd Maitland, "Books of the Season," *Minneapolis St. Paul* (June 1987): 188.

6. M. M. Mahood, ed., "Introduction" to *Twelfth Night* by William Shakespeare (New York: Viking Penguin, 1987), 131.

Chapter 4

1. Dag Hammarskjöld, *Markings*, trans. Leif Sjoberg (New York: Alfred A. Knopf, 1967).

2. See, for example, Robert J. Lifton, *Boundaries* (Toronto: CBC Publications, 1969).

Chapter 5

1. See John Newton, *Out of the Depths* (New Canaan, Conn.: Keats Publishing Company, 1981). First published in 1764, this is the autobiography of an Englishman who was converted from slave trader to noted London minister. "Amazing Grace" is his best known composition.

2. *The Confessions of St. Augustine*, bk. 7, chap. 5, trans. Rex Warner, trans. (New York: New American Library, 1968), 168.

3. The Reverend David Denny, quoted in *Desert Call* (Crestone, Colo.: The Spiritual Life Institute) 18 (Fall 1983): 6.

4. Thorstein Veblen, *The Theory of the Leisure Class: An Economic Study* (New York: Macmillan Co., 1899).

Chapter 6

1. "Letters to the Editor," *The Guardian* (9 June 1987).

2. Much of what follows immediately is developed at length in Chapters 2 ("Aging: Inhibiting Attitudes, Subtle Resources") and 3 ("Wise Hearts: Assenting to Ambiguities") in my book *Aging: A Time for New Learning* (Louisville: Westminster/John Knox Press, 1987).

3. Rainer Maria Rilke, *Letters to a Young Poet*. trans. M. D. Hertrer Norton (New York: W. W. Norton & Co. Inc., 1954), 35.

4. Robert Burns, "To a Louse," *The Poetical Works of Robert Burns* (Glasgow: David Bryce and Son, [n.d.]).

5. Amos Wilder, in *Early Christian Rhetoric: The Language of the Gospels* (New York: Harper and Row, 1964), argues that such was the novelty of the gospel that new literary forms had to be fashioned in order to express it. Old wineskins will not contain new wine. I suggest that *The Confessions* were a similar innovation in order that an emerging Christian individual might be able to enflesh his experience as one who had tried to live without God.

6. David J. Maitland, *Looking Both Ways: A Theology for Mid-Life* (Louisville: Westminster/John Knox Press, 1985).

Epilogue

1. Florida Scott-Maxwell, *The Measure of My Days* (New York: Alfred P. Knopf, 1973), 42.

2. Francis Parkman, *The Oregon Trail* (New York: The New American Library, Signet Classic, 1950), 72.

3. William Shakespeare, *King Henry IV*, bk. 2, act 5, sc.5, lines 50–63.

4. David J. Maitland, "Vocation," in M. P. Halverson, *A Handbook of Christian Theology* (New York: Meridian Books, 1958) 371f.